FOREKNOWN

Kent Ward Clark

PRESS

DEDICATION
AND
ACKNOWLEDGEMENTS

T his book is dedicated to the thousands of abused mothers and their children, who have sought shelter from the storms of life at Grace Centers of Hope and have found Christ to be their souls' harbor.

There are so many who have contributed to the writing of this allegory, but none spent as many hours reading and editing as Pat Yeakey. Thank you, Pat, for your untiring work in helping me bring the story to print.

Thank you to Scott Gillesby and Ray Holm for the financial support needed to print this and the other works to follow.

CONTENTS

The Middle of Life

On the surface, the two of us seemed to be a match made in heaven…and maybe we were. I was an honor roll student, homecoming queen and captain of our varsity cheerleading squad. Jack was our high school football team captain and played on the all-state team. As president of the Student Council, National Honor Society (straight A's in his senior year) and a leader in Voice of Christian Youth, he was 'Mr. High School' personified. Jack worked at a prestigious men's clothing store in our town and was always 'dressed to the nines', resulting in him being voted 'Best Dressed' in our senior year. We were crowned king and queen at the prom by our fellow students, who often referred to us as 'Ken & Barbie'. My man, Jack, had a wonderful heart-winning smile. He was 6'3" with wavy, coal-black hair, muscular, incredibly handsome and we were truly in love.

Early in life I knew men were drawn to my appearance and, believe me, I used it as the sharpest tool in my bag to get what I felt like I needed. I well remember times when men would smile, wink and silently mouth to me, *'You are beautiful'*—even when Jack was standing right next to me. I responded with nothing more than blushing cheeks and a shy smile. Secretly, it thrilled my heart and served as fuel to feed the fire for my need of approval. However, the shame I felt from the things I held deep within me always kept the compliments short lived.

The activities I was involved in during my high school years afforded me the opportunity to cover the deep, dark secret that was a constant shadow over my life. The cheerleading, being homecoming queen, dating Jack and in general trying to stay out of the house as much as I could all worked together to divert the pain in my heart. Jack didn't compliment me as much as other people—maybe because he was into himself to the same extent that I was into getting my own needs met. I loved Jack, but almost from the beginning I knew he didn't meet my deepest need. I was far too young to see that my need and his inability to supply it would be a fatal flaw in our relationship. Was there any man who could meet that need, who could be my shield and comfort?

Jack and I got married 20 years ago, fresh out of high school. We were so young—just 18 years of age and eagerly heading off to college. We had been sweethearts since the tenth grade when Jack's typing teacher, Mr. Providence, introduced us to each other one afternoon at the end of the school day. Jack won a contest in his fifth-hour typing class and <u>I</u> was the prize! Mr. Providence promised the guys in the class, which was largely comprised of our varsity football team, a formal introduction between me (his homeroom assistant) and the winner of the contest. Mr. Providence made the 'deal' without consulting me; but when I met the contest winner, any hesitation I may have had was set aside.

It seemed like love at first sight for both of us. Mr. Providence introduced us to each other as "Jack Elect" and "Foreknown". I vividly remember Jack's face turning as red as his shirt and I'm sure mine was a similar color. He asked for my phone number on the spot and called later that day wanting to know if I would go out with him the following Friday night. Being a cheerleader, I had been aware of Jack for some time…we just hadn't met until now. I was also aware that lots of my friends would have jumped at the chance to date him. So, when he asked, I didn't hesitate to accept and it turned out to be a perfect date. We went to our high school's basketball game, then to McDonald's for fries, Cokes and conversation. We talked about a lot of things, but Jack seemed guarded and it was clear to me he wasn't comfortable talking about himself. I guess because of the secrets in my own life, I remember wondering if he, too, was hiding something.

As our evening progressed, I realized Jack was a serious kind of guy with a fatherly air about him. The conversation flowed easily and freely, though, and eventually turned to talk of religion and God. I was thrilled to discover I was dating a Christian, yet a little apprehensive. What if our dating developed into something serious? What if Jack discovered the black secret in my life? Would he still love me? Could he forgive me or would he even understand? Then again, why should I care if I was dating a Christian? I wasn't sure I was a Christian myself. How could I be? Most of the time, I just felt contaminated and dirty.

Jack attended Graceville Reformed Baptist Church, which was very Calvinistic in its beliefs and well known for teaching the doctrine of 'predestination'. I attended Palestine Methodist Church, a congregation wanting nothing to do with that line of thinking. My pastor was very opposed to what he called the 'Tulip', saying it was a doctrine hatched in hell. When I heard him make such a strong statement, I had to ask about the 'Tulip' thing. He told me predestination believers used 'Tulip' as an acronym for their doctrinal beliefs:

'T' is for total depravity, meaning we are born in enmity against God, that we are haters of God from birth and our will is enslaved to our enmity nature.

'U' is for unconditional election, meaning that out of this enmity group, God has chosen a number of people no man can number who would be saved.

'L' is for limited atonement, meaning Christ has redeemed all of the enmity people God chose.

'I' is for irresistible grace, meaning the chosen enmity people shall be drawn to the Lord Jesus Christ by the Holy Spirit and this drawing is irresistible on the part of those chosen people.

'P' is for the perseverance of the saints, meaning all the chosen enmity people shall persevere to the end. They will get up when they fall, they cannot quit and they just keep on keeping on.

I especially liked the last point because, in spite of my black secret, I could never deny Christ was the Son of God.

Tulips have always been my favorite flower, but I've never been too sure about this religious brand of 'Tulip'. I must say, there have been times since meeting Jack and discussing our doctrinal differences that I've secretly wondered if these teachings are true—if there really is hope for me. Predestination people believe God has designed a master plan for everything and everyone. They also believe He is sovereign and His plan, which He purposed in Himself, shall surely come to pass because He predestined it. Predestination believers are big on this thing of a 'purpose-driven life'. I'm not sure I agree, but it would give me so much hope if God truly could, and did, work everything out for my good. I wonder, though, how God could take my black secret and work it for my good. Oh, I do hope He is powerful enough to do such a thing!

Thinking about our marriage I realize, for most of it, the doctrine of how God saves the sinner created moments, sometimes days, of coolness in our relationship. Jack was patient with me, though. I must admit he was a great teacher and would refer to scripture passages to make his point about the 'Tulip'. He would always end our conversation by saying, "Foreknown, all truth is revealed truth and I pray for you every day that God will reveal to you the truth of His free grace. Grace is such a comforting message. Just to know God loves us freely, without a cause <u>in</u> us or <u>about</u> us, is what gets me through the drudgery of this life." Usually, Jack's patience and persistent statements of 'revealed truth' only made the situation worse. Part of what Jack talked about rang true with me, though. There was something about this grace thing that <u>did</u> comfort me when I considered the black secret of my life.

But, I'm ahead of my story.

During our courtship, I can't say either of our churches was very supportive in the area of encouraging us to keep our bodies pure and unblemished of sexual sin. Maybe 'supportive' isn't the right word. In spite of the fact that neither of our churches overtly addressed abstaining from sexual contact until marriage, we all knew it was a 'no-no'. Both churches disapproved of dancing, the 'suggestion' being it would lead to sex—although my mind was never quite able to understand the connection between those two issues. There were other things they could have talked about that we should refrain from to keep ourselves pure. Instead, they 'cut on the limbs of the tree' rather than getting to the root of the issue. Jack and I had many discussions about 'saving ourselves' until our wedding night, only to end up surrendering to the overpowering lust of our flesh a short time later. For me, it didn't matter anyhow. Why was I even discussing 'saving myself' and for what? There was nothing to 'save'. Plus, that black secret was always there, hanging over me. Jack seemed to feel far more guilt than I did after we crossed the boundaries we had set for ourselves, although I never quite understood why. Was it possible he had secrets as well, or had my own secrets hardened me to the point where I was left with nothing but a seared conscience? I ended up reasoning with myself that none of it mattered, because we would be married eventually and the problem would be solved. Jack never questioned me about my virginity—I would have lied anyway if he'd asked.

I was, and guess I still am, confused about this whole sexual thing. Did God Himself come up with the idea of sex? How is all of this supposed to work out? Is God angry if I enjoy sex? All I've ever wanted is to just be loved.

There were other real-life issues, perhaps more important ones, our pastors simply didn't address—subjects that were taboo, but needed to be brought out into the open, subjects that would have shed light on the dark place in my life where secrets were kept. One of those real-life issues was sexual abuse. The awful possibility of that type of thing happening in or out of the church was something they never talked about, except, maybe, behind closed doors.

Over the years, I came to understand that the responsibility of an earthly father to his child is to emulate, or be a mirror image of, our Heavenly Father. My own father failed this responsibility. He was a prominent member of our church, the head of the deacon board, our pastor's best friend…and he was sexually abusing me. I lost my virginity to my dad before I reached 10 years of age. I was repeatedly raped by the man who was supposed to be my earthly protector, but who violated me; my shield from harm, who injured me; my 'White Knight', who had a black heart. I was just a child carrying burdens much too heavy for a child to bear. That horrible, unnatural violation, perpetrated on me by my own father, left me in a constant state of worry and fear. I remember wondering if I was the only child this was happening to. Were there others and, if so, who was caring for them? Did anybody love us? Did God love us? If He did, why didn't He do something about it? I was only 10 years old and already felt dirty, lonely and so terribly confused.

As time went on and the sexual abuse continued, I acquired many coping skills—self-learned ones that enabled me to make it from one day to the next. One of the things I struggled greatly with was the true word that describes what was taking place between my dad and me. It was a word my mind wanted to dance around and use other terms that didn't seem quite so harsh, words that somehow *softened* what my dad was doing to me. It was a word reserved for what adults did with each other, not with 10-year-old children. The word was……it was…...INTERCOURSE! My father forced INTERCOURSE on me—a young, innocent child, a virgin who knew nothing of those things!

In the midst of the nightmare, however, a part of that little girl was getting something out of that unnatural relationship with her father. As horrible as it sounds to me now, at the time he made me feel special. He would kiss me, then tell me I was "beautiful" and that I was his "little girl". He said we had a secret only the two of us knew. I felt his approval and acceptance, things any little girl wants from her dad, but not in the sick, twisted way he was getting those messages across to me. I had no way of knowing those early-life experiences was to determine a path I would follow for the rest of my life.

The relationship between Jack and me during the time we dated rapidly deteriorated to nothing more than a physical one. What had started out as something sweet and innocent was now all about sex; and the more we allowed our flesh to take over, the more distant we became with one another. There was very little joy anymore, very little communication or fellowship, very little tenderness. There was just sex. Middle ground didn't exist with us. If we weren't having sex, we were fighting. Jack just seemed to be angry most of time and I didn't understand why.

I don't know. Maybe it was my own guilt tormenting me, but at some point I began to sense Jack was going to walk away from our relationship. I knew I couldn't let that happen. I loved Jack and needed him—I just wasn't sure which of the two was greater. I truly am, and always have been, a weak vessel.

When I began to seriously believe Jack was going to break off our relationship, a scheme came too easily to my mind—one that would back him into a corner and keep him in my life. My reasoning told me, even if he didn't love me, he would be bound by his principles to put a ring on my finger...*if I was pregnant.* I knew, in

Jack's mind, he would have no choice but to marry me. He was just that kind of guy. So, I made the decision and formulated a plan.

Both sets of parents were leaving for an out-of-town trip for three or four days and had assured themselves we were old enough, responsible enough, mature enough and 'Christian' enough to conduct ourselves in a proper manner. So, our families left the two of us to our own devices. I can't imagine what Jack's parents could have been thinking! I guess they simply trusted us. As for my parents, my father *had* to know Jack and I were intimate with each other. I'm sure my mother knew as well. She was *very* aware of such things. She, too, was a part of my black secret, because she looked the other way regarding what was happening to her daughter and chose my dad over me. None of them, however, had any way of knowing that <u>nothing</u> could deter me from doing what I felt I had to do—not the dark secret of my past nor the confusion and desire of the present.

My plan was to have Jack come over to our house one night so we could be "completely alone with no interruptions", which is exactly how I said it when I invited him. I made sure the message was clear and the offer was too irresistible for him to refuse. We both knew how our evening would end—the way most of our private time together ended. When I asked him, Jack grinned sheepishly and said, "Of course, I'll be there. That's an opportunity I can't pass up." He came to me that night, an eager and willing participant. Unfortunately, he had no way of knowing I had an ulterior motive and that it was part of a trap. The first step of the scheme to make sure Jack stayed in my life couldn't have been easier. Everything went smoothly.

When we found out a month later I was pregnant, the torrent of guilt and panic we felt was almost unbearable. For obvious reasons we were frightened and worried. Not the least of those reasons was that Jack's father was the pastor of Graceville Reformed Baptist Church, which had a large congregation in our little town. My own father, my perpetrator, was a deacon at our small church, Palestine Methodist. Even though I planned the entrapment and felt I had thought things through carefully, I guess I hadn't counted on the awful emotions I was experiencing. I remember thinking: *What if Jack figures out this whole thing wasn't an accident and I had purposed for it to happen? What if he really doesn't love me?* I realize now that, even back then, my thought processes and decisions were all about me.

Jack was so distraught over the pregnancy there were moments when I feared he would take his life. Looking back on it, I think that was the beginning of his health problems. The doctors told him his stomach issues were psychosomatic. It irritated Jack to no end when the doctors said his *symptoms* were real, but the *problem* was in his mind, not his stomach. He tried to control everything, but stress was one thing Jack couldn't control. Secrets make you sick…and keep you sick. I believe the church has passively taught Christians to put on a façade of being holy and some of their followers have become very good at it. Preacher's kids, you know, are supposed to be the 'super good' kids. Jack says he was told at an early age by his grandmother that he had to be a good boy or he would ruin his dad's ministry. (I remember kidding Jack and telling him he was a <u>bad</u> boy because he was hanging out with the deacon's daughter!) Jack agonized over what the pregnancy would do to his father's ministry. What would the deacons say? What would their church do?

Graceville Reformed had its peculiarities. Not only were they predestination people, but in some areas I thought they were as legalistic as the Methodist denomination. There seemed to be an unspoken part of us the whole religious experience couldn't conquer. Both churches, I thought, were full of pretense and totally ignored, or simply didn't address in a straightforward manner, the issues of real life. I know in my particular situation there was no voice in either church that addressed my black secret or even made mention of the possibility of it existing. There were other things that bothered me, too…simple things. When Jack was captain of the high school football team, he was never allowed to go to practice wearing shorts in the August heat like the rest of the players. 'Indecency' was the reason given. He couldn't play basketball either because of the uni-forms. What was it about wearing a basketball uniform that was so ungodly? It seemed to me everything they claimed was 'evil', they also somehow managed to connect to sex. Jack's dad believed dancing was immoral, so I could only imagine what would happen when they found out I was pregnant. My own dad would have prob-ably been satisfied with a quick wedding and a baby in six months.

I don't think he would have been terribly upset, as it would have helped divert any suspicion of wrongdoing away from him.

Having been molested in the most degrading way by my deacon father severely impacted my perception of a Father God. There were moments when I felt special to my dad, but dirty and sick at the same time. How confusing it all was. Could this Father God be like my dad, at times loving and at other times so unjust? What a mess! How can all this happen to people who are professing to know God? Who is this God who loves sinners? Does He love them, yet abuse them? If He loves me, where was He all those years when my own father was molesting me? Is God really more concerned about Jack's legs being exposed by wearing a basketball uniform than about my own father raping me?!

As the weeks flew by and the reality of my pregnancy set in, I could see Jack was becoming depressed. He was distant and despondent. I couldn't escape the realization of being responsible for this terrible mess, so I made another decision—one I thought would correct it. I scheduled an appointment with a doctor and went alone so no one would *ever* know.

The abortion clinic was located in a city just fifty miles from our small town. I got up that morning and went through my usual routine, as I didn't want anyone to suspect something was out of the ordinary. I drove to the address that was given to me, but wasn't sure it was the right place. The building looked more like a high rise office building than an abortion clinic. No one would guess this was a place where tiny, innocent lives were being vacuumed from their quiet resting places. Walking into the clinic, one would think you had entered the office of my family physician. What a facade this place presented to the weaker vessels who came for the services rendered here.

After filling out the necessary paperwork, I was told to have a seat. As I looked around the room, most of the women there that day were much older than I and a thought went through my mind that we probably had very little in common. Then I realized, at that moment in time we all shared at least one thing…we were there to get rid of something that wasn't going to fit into our lives in one way or another. The looks on their faces told me they were experiencing the same feeling I was and wishing they didn't have to be doing 'this'. (Yet, another word I couldn't say at that point.)

When my turn came, the nurse called my name and motioned for me to follow her into a room already set up for the procedure. Soon, Dr. Slaughter came in, introduced himself and proceeded to explain how he would terminate the pregnancy by sucking the fetus from my womb with a powerful vacuum. I was lightly sedated, but it didn't keep me from hearing and feeling that tiny life being torn from inside me.

In less than forty-five minutes everything was over and I was moved to a holding area where Dr. Slaughter spoke briefly with me. He said my pregnancy was farther along than I had thought. He told me it was a male, but there was something unhealthy about the fetus—that it had a greenish color to it, which indicated it was unlikely I would have carried it to full term. None of this was of any comfort to me, however. I just wanted to get out of there, back to my little town and into Jack's arms.

A few hours later, I was home and the problem had been solved—or so I thought. I will never forget the flood of relief that washed over Jack's face when I lied to him. "There is no pregnancy, Jack. I lost the baby." He asked very few questions, but it was clearly evident the burden he had been carrying was now gone. In all our years together I never told him anything other than what I did that day.

Jack and I continued to date and did our best to resist getting overly intimate with each other. It never got any easier, but I think the fear of another pregnancy helped us make it through our senior year.

As I've said, Jack and I got married right after graduation. Because my dad was having financial problems at the time, he wanted me to wear my aunt's wedding dress to help reduce the expenses. Jack was having no part of that, however, so he bought my dress. Not knowing my black secret, he said to me, "Even though you and I have already had intercourse, you were *my* virgin and I want you to wear a white dress."

As a little girl, when I would disassociate from what my dad was doing to me, I had visions of a beautiful, tall, elegant lady with flowing blond hair walking down the church aisle, eyes locked on her 'Prince Charming', who was waiting at the end for her. It didn't take me long to find the exact dress I had always envisioned. It was strapless, with a fitted bodice that went full from the waist down and flowed into a beautiful long train. It was perfect for my body and gracefully accented all my curves, including my tiny waist, which Jack had admired from the beginning. It was, truly, the dress of my dreams! My veil was floor length, edged in satin and the perfect accompaniment to the dress.

Our wedding day came and Mom was in the room where my bridesmaids and I were getting ready, trying to do whatever was needed to be helpful. After I slipped my dress on, she put my head-piece in place, straightening the veil. As we both turned to look in the mirror, she said, "Foreknown, you look so beautiful"; then she kissed me on the cheek, lifted the short part of my veil and lowered it over my face, which symbolized that I was a virgin. At that moment, as Mom and I stared into each other's eyes, any doubts I may have had that she knew what took place between Dad and me dissipated. No words were spoken and the black secret continued to be played out. The knock on the dressing room door told me Dad was waiting and it was time for him to give me away.

Dad and I walked up the steps from the lobby of the church to the main floor and waited at the beginning of the aisle. As the 'Wedding March' began to play, he took my hand, placed it around his arm and whispered to me, "Foreknown, you know, *you can never come home to me again.*" I smiled and we stepped into the church auditorium.

As the two of us began to walk, the words my father had just whispered in my ear found their way to my mind. In an instant, I felt their impact. Thoughts began to explode in my head like fire-crackers as I realized the years of sexual abuse at the hands of my father would finally be over when I reached the end of this aisle! An indescribable, overwhelming flood of relief washed over me and my legs grew so weak I thought I would collapse! I wanted to stop walking and let the truth of this feeling soak into every ounce of my being...but I knew I couldn't. I just kept moving forward and smiling, as another thought immediately followed the first. Suddenly, the wave of relief I had experienced was brutally swept away by anger—anger for what he *did* to me and anger for what he had just *said* to me! Once again, I felt used, abused and now thrown away by the man who should have loved and protected me as a child! I wanted to pound my fists on his chest! I wanted to shout and tell everyone in that auditorium who this man really was and what he had done to his daughter for eight years! But, I couldn't. He *knew* our dark secret was safe with me and that I would never tell.

As I forced my mind back into the moment, I realized we had only taken a couple of steps and still had a long walk ahead of us. Everything in me wanted to let go of my dad's arm and run as fast as I could to Jack—the man who was going to be my *real* 'White Knight', the man who would love me and protect me and meet my every need! At the end of the aisle I would finally be safe! But, of course, I didn't let go. I did what I had learned as a young girl—to just keep putting one foot in front of another.

By the time we reached where Jack was waiting, tears were stinging my eyes so badly I could hardly see. Jack's dad asked, "Who gives this woman in marriage?" My dad answered, "Her mother and I." Dad then took my hand and placed it in Jack's. In an instant I passed from one chapter of my life into the next. The two men in my life, Jack and my dad, were a mere three feet apart and both of them were touching me. It was a very confusing moment. I remember thinking, *I love them both, but in ways that are worlds apart.*

My emotions had reached such a peak that I cried during the entire wedding, at one point prompting a whisper from Jack's dad encouraging me to compose myself. His effort was futile. Too many thoughts and feelings had been released and the tears were impossible to hold back.

My father-in-law did a wonderful job performing our ceremony, which was beautiful and filled with lots of 'Tulip' overtones. Jack's dad spoke about God's providence—how, in His sovereignty, He drew us to one another and had a purpose for bringing us into the marriage. It seemed right even to me and I was reassured to think God had actually planned for us to be together. I remember promising Jack and the Lord that I, by the grace of our Lord Jesus Christ, would be a faithful wife to my husband. I would love him in sickness or in health, in poverty or in wealth. What condemnation those words bring to my remembrance, for I have kept none of my well-intentioned vows.

Jack and I settled into a little house my dad owned and began our life together. After much discussion about where to go to church, and much resistance on my part, we decided to attend Graceville Reformed Baptist, where my father-in-law was the pastor. (At that point, the only knowledge I had of anything being 'reformed' was reform school, and I sure didn't want any part of that!) It seemed to me Jack's dad was a little dogmatic on the issue of being a Baptist. Sometimes I got the feeling he was implying they would have the best seats in Heaven! I got very upset on several occasions when he said anyone who was 'sprinkled' had never been 'scripturally' baptized. The Baptist method is to put you completely under the water, as if they are burying you. Jack's dad said you can't represent a death, burial and resurrection by sprinkling holy water on a person's head. He would always illustrate his point by telling a story about the Methodist preacher's son who had a pet duck. One day the duck got choked on something and died. The little boy was heartbroken but wanted to conduct a funeral and bury the duck in the woods behind their home. "Ok, son, you go ahead and bury the duck yourself," said the boy's father. In preparation for the funeral, the little boy took his Bible, along with the 'casket', which was a shoebox with the duck inside, and headed to the woods. It wasn't very long until the little boy was back playing in his front yard.

After a few days, a terrible odor began to radiate from the woods. The Methodist preacher asked the boy, "Son, did you bury that duck?" "Yes, daddy," said the little boy, "just like you bury people in baptism when you sprinkle water on them. I sprinkled some dirt on that duck's head." When my father-in-law told that story, everyone in the congregation would laugh...except for me. I didn't think it was funny and I certainly got his point.

I was often confused and frightened by the sermons I heard at Graceville Reformed Baptist Church concerning the 'Judgment Seat of Christ'. Sometimes, it seemed to me there were two messages coming from the pulpit—one of grace, mercy and forgiveness, another of law, works and self effort. I thought it to be a strange mixture and found myself totally frustrated over the issue. In reality, though, it haunted me.

I remember a visiting pastor coming to the church and preaching four sermons on how all Christians will one day stand before God and give an account of everything they had ever done since being converted. The second night of his series he painted a vivid picture of God taking every Christian, one at a time, and standing them before the 'Judgment Seat'. The preacher said God was then going to play a video of each person's life on a big screen that showed everything they had done in their lives...good and bad. I can't tell you the horror I felt in my soul! The awful condemnation that ate at me caused excruciating pain. I was converted at the age of ten, which was around the time my dad started molesting me. He said it was our secret and if I ever told Mom, she wouldn't believe me. He said I would be responsible for breaking up our family. How cruel this God must be to reveal something in Heaven that, as a little girl, I was told to keep secret—something I had no control over, something forced on me, something that wasn't my fault!

Because I was so unsettled, on our way home from church I asked Jack, "Do you believe what the preacher said tonight?" Jack answered with "If it's true, I'm in a lot of trouble!" What he said was somewhat comforting, as it told me he didn't see how a message of condemnation fit into the gospel of unmerited favor and he, too, had some issues tucked away from the view of everyone but God Himself.

The third message of the series was no better than the first two. The preacher spoke about how every Christian is going to be rewarded according to his or her 'works'. Some Christians would be driving Cadillacs in Heaven, while others would be driving Fords. Some, he said, would live in "Heaven's 'hood", while others would live on "Main Street, New Jerusalem".

When we got home that evening, Jack said, "We won't be going to church tomorrow night. I'm taking you out to dinner." It was clear he had heard enough and wanted to shield me from a message void of grace. At that moment, I had such tender, loving thoughts toward Jack, realizing he knew this was not something good for me to hear and he was trying to protect me.

My father-in-law later apologized to the entire church for inviting that man and for the sermons he preached. I really could see how it was not consistent with the message of grace, which Jack's dad believed so fervently. There was something about the preacher's talk of appearing before the 'Judgment Seat', though, that caused me to write scripture verses in the back of my Bible — verses like, "But by the grace of God I am what I am"; "For it is God which worketh IN YOU both to will and to do of His good pleasure"; "their sins and their iniquities will I remember no more"; "As far as the east is from the west, so far hath He removed our transgressions from us"; "for thou hast cast all my sins behind thy back."

There were times when I asked Jack what his thoughts were about Heaven and whether he thought we would live in "Heaven's 'hood" or "Main Street, New Jerusalem". He'd answer with, "Baby, I don't care whether it's 'Heaven's 'hood' or Heaven's 'Main Street'. Just for us to be there will be GLORY!" Then he would quote, " 'For whom HE did FOREKNOW, HE also did PREDESTINATE... whom HE did PREDESTINATE, them HE also CALLED: and whom HE CALLED, them HE also JUSTIFIED: and whom HE JUSTIFIED, them HE also GLORIFIED.' Remember, Foreknown, 'we are His workmanship, created in Christ Jesus unto good works, which God hath before ordained that we should walk in them.' I know, Foreknown, it is grace that puts us in the way, leads us along the way and takes us all the way." I loved it when Jack talked to me like that. He sounded so confident and strong in his beliefs.

During high school, Jack had taken vocational training and was a star pupil in their carpentry program. After we were married, he decided he wouldn't go to college, but would get his builder's license and start his own construction company, which he named 'Grace Builders, Inc.' Jack was skilled, the timing was perfect, the housing market was booming and his business took off like a rocket. While he worked, I started night school at a community college, taking classes with the hope of one day becoming a social worker.

Jack and I saw very little of each other the first year of our marriage. Most evenings he would just be getting home from work as I was rushing out for my classes. I had always believed people get married to live together, to be together. That wasn't happening and it made me realize my needs had never changed. There was still an empty hole in my heart needing to be filled and I desperately wanted Jack to fill it, but he seemingly couldn't—or maybe he just wouldn't. I longed for Jack, my 'White Knight', to take my hand, tell me I was his girl and kiss me. I longed to be held and told I was beautiful. Instead, Jack and I grew farther apart—or maybe it was me who pulled away from him. I don't know. There was also the possibility it was only in my mind. I wondered what was in Jack's mind. How could he let us grow apart like this? He should have been more of a spiritual leader in our marriage. I wish we had talked more or he had seen what was taking place and put a stop to it.

Jack's stomach problems continued to get worse. The doctors were telling him he had something they referred to as 'builder's stomach'. Jack said he was familiar with the term and that most contractors constantly took Rolaids because of the problems and stresses involved in building houses. I wasn't sure, though, that building houses was the reason Jack felt sick. I only know the two of us just kept living our lives on slowly-emerging, separate paths.

There was a man in one of my night classes who actually attended our church and sang in the choir. He was older, but still very attractive. We began to talk a lot before class and I soon found myself trying to arrive early just so I could spend a few minutes with him. He was pleasant and engaging...and married. In my mind I reasoned there was nothing wrong with the two of us just talking—after all, it *was* a public place. Often, our conversation found its way to discussions about our church and its message. He wasn't a real believer in the sovereignty of God. If that was true, I wondered why he even attended our church. Also, Jack's dad was not his favorite person. There were times when I felt he crossed a line in his criticism of my father-in-law and his teaching. He seemed to dislike the message, though, more than the messenger.

'Choir Man' was kind and attentive to me and the fact that we were both married didn't seem to matter to him. I did have some strange feelings, though, when he talked about his wife. It almost seemed like he was saying in a round-about way she really wouldn't care if he was involved with another woman. I remember thinking how it would have torn me up if I found out Jack was pursuing someone else. Then I realized how strange it was for me to think like that when I had been totally unfaithful to him in so many ways.

One night, during a fifteen-minute classroom break, 'Choir Man' invited me to join him for a cup of coffee…and I did. It was then I began to realize a connection was taking place between the two of us. I knew somewhere in my heart that a continued friendship would lead to trouble, but I had no desire to turn down the invitation each time he asked. My self-centered needs controlled me like a person hooked on heroin. Many times my guilt would overwhelm me and I would say to him, "This doesn't feel right. It has to stop." Both of us knew what was happening and what it would lead to, but the lines had already been crossed. I told him I wanted to serve God and we just should not continue this way. He would always agree, but our relationship had gone too far. He had already begun to tell me he couldn't live without me. He would hold me in his arms and I'd kiss him as if I'd never said anything about thinking this was wrong. At times, it was almost a feeling of being under an other-worldly influence—that 'Choir Man' had some sort of control over me. I quickly set that feeling aside, as he was gentle, kind, tender and fun loving—all the things a woman desires. I had guilt, but I was good at the self-talk thing and convinced myself nothing terribly wrong would come of our relationship. *I can stop this at any time. We've done nothing more than kiss and Jack will never know. Jack isn't giving you what you need anyhow. 'Choir Man' is filling your need.* I was turning into an adulteress!

What was wrong with me? How could I be a Christian and keep up this constant flirtation and unfaithfulness? Could the 'Tulip' people be right about God loving us freely? I just knew there could be nothing in me that would move the heart of God to love me. In my Methodist church, I was told the 'Tulip' people believe you can sin all you want and still go to heaven. The more I continued in my self-indulgent ways, the more I knew the 'Tulip' people's beliefs couldn't be right if, indeed, they did teach that doctrine. *Let us sin that grace may abound!* Is that what I was saying? No, I didn't believe that. Surely a converted person could not live the kind of life I was living and expect to go to Heaven. The 'Tulip' people are wrong. But was I saying, then, that I'm going to hell? I abhorred myself! There was no trusting in my own heart, no inherent righteousness in me and I knew it. I had heard Jack's dad say a thousand times, "It is impossible to go from no faith to faith with no change."

What was it with me? The very thought of seeing 'Choir Man' made me giddy and almost childish with excitement. One night, he suggested we skip class and have dinner at the Marriott. By then, I had reached the point where I was more than willing to go with him. There is something about a man and a woman sharing a meal that creates a bond and 'Choir Man' knew it. After a very romantic dinner, he asked if we could spend some time together…alone. He told me he had reserved a room, promising he would behave himself. He said it would be quieter there and we could talk. I knew better. You don't go to a hotel room to 'talk'. But I laughed and said,

"Only if you keep your promise." I was calm on the outside, but inside a rush of adrenaline, coursing through every part of my body, filled me with an excitement I had never experienced. I willingly got on the elevator with him. There was barely a passing thought of Jack, my vows, my God. 'Choir Man' made no attempt to keep his promise and I did nothing to resist him. My cup was empty. I was thirsty and wanted to drink fully and deeply.

I had done it again—given in to another temptation after all the thoughts I'd had about my relationship with God. I decided I must be mentally ill. How could I live with myself after that night? But 'that night' continued to repeat itself. Each time after we were together, I would go home to my trusting husband and my lover to his wife.

The Sunday following one of our trysts, Jack's father preached and there, sitting in the choir loft right behind him, was my lover. The text for my father-in-law's sermon was taken from Hosea, chapter 14, verse 4, where God says, "I will love them freely". He then began telling the story of Hosea and Gomer. In the sermon, my father-in-law used Hosea to represent God and Gomer to represent the church. God, it seems, told Hosea to marry a prostitute named Gomer. The scripture says, after marrying Hosea, Gomer periodically left her husband and went to her lovers; but Hosea always sent his servants to watch over her. When Gomer was found in need, Hosea, through his servant, would supply whatever her needs were. Whether it was food, clothing or shelter, Hosea made sure she was taken care of. Gomer would return home each time, only to leave again. When she left for the third time, she was gone for years and grew old away from her husband. Through all her days away from him, though, Hosea had supplied her every need. Finally, the word came back to Hosea that she was on prostitute row downtown.

As I sat listening to my father-in-law's message, I began to sob uncontrollably. I realized I was Gomer! Thinking 'Choir Man' would be fearful I was having a breakdown and wondering if I was going to confess, I glanced at him expecting to see a worried face—but he almost seemed to be smirking at me! His expression was very unsettling. Jack put his arm around my shoulders, trying to console me. In a way I can't explain, it almost felt like I was being consoled by the Comforter Himself as I listened to this amazing account of the truth of God's grace. Jack's dad continued the story by telling what happened when the servant came back with the news that Gomer was old, ugly, wrinkled and on prostitute row. Amazingly, Hosea went to where she was!

In Biblical times the pimps lined up their prostitutes according to youth and beauty. When Hosea reached where Gomer was, he met the pimp, who attempted to sell him a prostitute from the group that was young and beautiful. Hosea walked down the line until he reached the end and there was Gomer…old, dirty, wrinkled, sick and forlorn. To the pimp's amazement, Hosea said, "I want her. I will purchase her and love her freely." At that moment, something inside of me cried out: *This is grace! This is amazing grace!* But was this grace for me? Then, from my heart, came another cry: *Oh,*

God, what have I done? The 'black dog' in my soul barked ever so loudly that night. Again, I had been "allured and brought into a wilderness". Surely, Almighty God would pour out the condemnation on me I so deserved!

Because of the total meltdown I had that Sunday, I assumed Jack knew something was wrong, but couldn't put his finger on it—or maybe I just thought he couldn't. His demeanor revealed he was having some internal struggles of his own. As for me, I was often irritable and purposely started arguments with him. When we made love, I felt especially close to him, yet so very guilty. There were times when Jack seemed angry during our lovemaking. Maybe it was my imagination and guilt, but I felt there was something other than love taking place—that it was just sex on his part. I wondered if Jack was having a love/hate relationship with me. He would often say, "We never solve any issues between us. They're always just left out there hanging." I pretended not to know what he was talking about…but I did. I was a liar personified. I remember my mother asking me, "Foreknown, why are you constantly lying?" I was able to go into such a state of denial that lies became truth and I sometimes wondered if I had multiple personalities. There were times when my ability to justify, to live as if something didn't happen, frightened me. Jack knew I was lying and wasn't going to be satisfied with anything but the truth. I think he also knew he wouldn't get it. When Jack pressured me, like any red-blooded husband would who suspected his wife of cheating, I always shifted the blame to him. I was a master at manipulation and would have Jack feeling like he was less than a loving husband before the conversation ended. Many times I saw the pain in his eyes and knew, to some degree, I was contributing to his physical illness.

Jack's health problems grew worse. He was constantly seeing a doctor, whose answer to all of Jack's symptoms—the chest pain, headaches, earaches and stomach problems—was always the same: psychosomatic. *How could I do this to the man I love? My heart is so full of pollution there is no hope for me. I could make Jack physically well again if I would only be truthful with him. It would be a bitter pill for him to swallow, but he would forgive me...he loved me.* Oh, how I prayed for the grace to stop my evil, self-centered behavior.

Well into the affair with 'Choir Man', I had no period for two months in a row. I was hopeful stress had caused this lapse in my cycle, but it wasn't to be. I was pregnant and didn't know who the father was—my husband or my lover. I knew I couldn't take the risk of having a child that might not be Jack's. What if he discovered the truth? I told neither my husband nor my lover about the pregnancy. It was so difficult for me to deal with, but I found myself back at the most dreaded place on earth to me...the abortion clinic. Dr. Slaughter recognized me and proceeded to give me a much-needed lecture on birth control. He asked if my husband was in the waiting room and seemed somewhat irritated when I told him Jack had to work. I remember thinking: *You're assisting me in murdering my baby then lecturing me about the virtues of a good husband and birth control!* How fickle we all are when it comes to our moral judgments. We commit our own grievous sins, then judge others for lesser violations. Is it a cover up? Is that why we point the finger, to distract others from looking our way? Jack's father says the list of morals from churches is like horse manure and cow manure—they're both manure, just different kinds. The whole world with its religion looked like one big mess to me. Is that what Jack's father meant when he spoke of the total depravity of man? So there I was, having my second abortion within a three-year time span. When it was over, I once again headed home...back to Jack.

Soon after that second abortion, I dropped out of college and cut off all communication with my lover. True, I saw him at church, but I acted as though we'd never met. If he cared for me at all, he had to be tormented. Secretly, I wanted to believe he was tormented. There was something about him wanting me that gave me a 'rush'. I figured there was no hope for me and I was utterly perverted and wicked. The 'Tulip' people sure have the 'T' right...total depravity! How could I do all I'd done—use people, cheat, lie—and still call myself a child of God?

The days and months passed quickly. Jack's business grew and he became a very successful builder. We were now financially able to leave the little two-bedroom house my dad owned and buy one ourselves. It was a relief to finally be out from under that last little bit of his control. Jack designed and built us a large house in an upscale neighborhood. It was everything a woman could wish for—five bedrooms, three baths, even a swimming pool in the backyard. Jack left nothing out.

The very first day in our new house our next-door neighbors, Leonard, Sharon and their two little girls, came over to introduce themselves and welcome us to the neighborhood. We discovered they were Christians and about our age. Jack and I really enjoyed talking with them and appreciated their welcome-to-the-neighborhood visit. We knew immediately we would soon be close friends.

Sharon and I bonded instantly and quickly realized we were soul mates. Sharing a pot of coffee every day after she sent her children off to school immediately became a morning ritual. We shopped, exercised, went to lunch, talked about our families and at times voiced critical remarks about our husbands and their lack of understanding our needs.

Leonard and Sharon attended Mt. Sinai Missionary Baptist Church, a very strict church outside our little town. One morning, Sharon and I began discussing the subject of religion. Our churches were the same denomination, but the only similarity between them was the word 'Baptist'. Sharon's church majored on the do's and don'ts of life. She was very well-versed in the rules and obeyed them. She didn't smoke, drink alcohol, dance or play cards. Once I asked her if she'd like to go to an afternoon movie and she quickly let me know movies were another 'forbidden' in her church. Sharon only wore skirts, because her church taught that pants were men's apparel and "the Bible forbids women from wearing anything that looks manly". Somehow our conversations about religion always managed to find their way back to her church's rules—and there were a lot of them. It seemed to me Sharon knew all about the rules in her church but had little knowledge about the Bible itself.

Sharon had beautiful, long, black hair, which she said had never been cut. She told me her dad showed her in the Bible, I think from I or II Corinthians, that only prostitutes cut their hair. She said long hair was her 'covering' and signified she was in subjection to her husband. "It's in the Bible," she said.

During that conversation with Sharon, thoughts crept into my mind of a haircut I had as a young girl, probably around age 12. My mother was very angry with me one day but wouldn't tell me why. She grabbed me by the shoulders, pushed me down hard onto the seat of a chair, took a pair of scissors and began to haphazardly whack away, throwing handfuls of my beautiful hair in a pile on the floor. After she finished and left the room, I looked at myself in a mirror, horrified at what was looking back at me! My mother had cut my hair so short there were several places where my scalp was exposed! I sobbed and begged her to let me stay home from school since I knew class pictures were being taken the next day. She knew it, too. My heartbroken pleas fell on deaf ears, though. She made me go. Needless to say, when the pictures came in a few weeks later, they were horrible. My mother bought them anyhow. Over the years, whenever I saw those pictures they served as reminders of a frightening day in my life when something happened to me that I didn't understand—another incident added to my long list of things that are impossible for a child's mind to reason out.

I remember Jack's dad preaching a sermon once entitled, "The One Rule", which was taken from Galatians 6:16, "And as many as walk according to this rule, peace be on them, and mercy, and upon the Israel of God." Jack's dad said, "The RULE the Apostle Paul was talking about was found in verse 14 of the same chapter: 'But God forbid that I should glory, save in the cross of our Lord Jesus Christ…'". I guess I have clung to that one RULE because in it I find my only hope.

As the days and months passed, Sharon and I became almost inseparable. When the four of us went out to dinner, Jack and Leonard often teased us about the amount of time we spent together. Over time, Sharon and I gained each other's confidence and began sharing a lot of personal things, although I did draw the line at telling her my black secret. I felt if I told her about being molested by my father she would think of me as 'dirty', since she had been raised in such a hard, cold, religious family.

One morning while we were having coffee, Sharon began to really open up and shared with me how she never knew a father's love. I certainly could identify with her in that area. Her father was an ordained Baptist minister, although he was only a pastor for a few years at a small independent Baptist church until being forced to leave. Sharon said her church was always in a squabble about something. She vividly recalled one Wednesday night at the monthly business meeting when the congregation actually voted to remove her dad from his position as pastor. The situation escalated to a point where the sheriff had to be called to prevent church members from trying to kill one another! Sharon said she had no enjoyable memories of church and the only reason she still went was because she feared going to hell more than going to church!

At one point during our conversation, Sharon reached over, took my hand and said, "But I enjoy so much being with you." Still holding my hand, she went on to tell me about her very dominant, strict, religious mother, who never showed a tender side. Sharon said it was like having two adult males in the house. "My mother ran the show in spite of the fact that my dad was a preacher. He was hard and stern, but no match for my mom. They argued a lot, but my mom always had the upper hand," she said. A thought went through my mind: *I wonder if Sharon's mom had long hair, too. Obviously, 'subjection' to her husband wasn't part of her religion!*

We sat and talked about the years of subtle abuse from our overtly-religious parents—who, with all their talk of God, didn't have a clue about raising a child in an atmosphere of God's grace. *God's grace*, I thought. *Do I know the grace of God? Maybe.*

At this point, I sensed something surfacing in both of us—something overwhelming and unstoppable. Suddenly, tears began to flow from Sharon as if a mighty torrent was about to release itself. I leaned over, wrapped my arms around her and held her as the floodgate of her emotions opened. She put her arms around me and sobbed uncontrollably. As we sat there, holding each other, thoughts of all my own problems and unfaithfulness to Jack were racing through my mind. Still, there was a sense within me that I was loved by Father God. It's strange how emotional feelings, even sexual feelings, are so close to spiritual feelings. *I'm learning I can't trust my feelings, which makes me feel even _more_ alone and helpless*. I loved Sharon and my heart went out to her, but I was totally unprepared for what was about to happen.

We both had been weeping, Sharon uncontrollably. When she finally began to calm down, I relaxed my arms a little and leaned back. As we looked into each other's eyes, I gently brushed the tears from her face with my hand and told her I loved her. She responded, "I love you, too."

Which one of us made the next move, I don't know. The kiss we shared was sweet and tender. During those few seconds, a thousand disturbing thoughts traveled through the brain links of my mind. I felt a deep emotional bond with Sharon and I can't honestly say I didn't feel some kind of sensual pleasure, but I quickly withdrew from the embrace.

Sharon was the first to speak. "Foreknown, I love you. What I mean is…I am really in love with you. I have been fighting this for months. I have never known the tenderness, the bonding, the understanding and the oneness we have. I don't believe there is anybody in the world like you. You feel the same, don't you? I know you do."

"Sharon," I said, "I do care deeply for you. In many ways I am attracted to you and feel drawn to you. Thank you for loving me." We both giggled like school girls, then gave each other a hug and a quick peck on the lips.

The mood changed and we began to talk about future plans as if nothing had happened between us. I think Sharon mistook my not confronting her with what had just taken place to be the answer to her question and that my feelings for her were mutual. I didn't confront her because I was afraid of losing my best friend. It was another very confusing moment in time. I couldn't ignore the sensual feelings I'd experienced either, which only served to compound my confusion.

This was the first, but certainly not the last, of many physically tender moments between the two of us. Sharon was much more aggressive when it came to wanting the physical and sexual contact. I didn't believe I was a lesbian, but the feelings I was having were complicated and confusing. There was something I was getting from my relationship with Sharon, something I didn't get from Jack or my ex-lover, 'Choir Man'. Sharon and I met each other's need for tenderness and understanding. She would often say to me, "Foreknown, if you will just let yourself love me, just give yourself permission, it'll be all right. I've been attracted to women for as long as I can remember. There's just no comparison between being loved by a woman and being loved by a man. I can give you the tenderness you long for. Jack can't give you what I can. What has he ever done for you anyway? You've shared so much with me about your unhappiness with him. Just leave him. You can make it on your own—we can make it together."

Sharon definitely touched a special place within me that neither Jack nor my ex-lover had been able to reach. The need I felt coming from that place made me wonder if there was truth in her words. Sharon had had many affairs with women and knew of course about my own indiscretion. I couldn't help but think: *Sharon doesn't drink or smoke but is totally lost in ungodly sexuality.* But so was I! I wondered if we were the only two women professing faith and involved in local churches, yet struggling with such twisted, hell-bent issues. I thought about our church backgrounds—Sharon, a legalistic, independent Baptist, and me, Mrs. Foreknown Elect, in the Calvinistic Reformed Baptist Church. There really wasn't any difference between Sharon and me. We both deserved the wrath of God!

There's a verse in the Bible somewhere (I've heard Jack's dad read it and quote it many times) that says, "For who maketh thee to differ from another?" I constantly had contradictory thoughts bumping into one another inside my head. *I know I'm not a lesbian. I know, too, I could have been and am humbled that I'm not. I also know I'm an adulterer and no better than Sharon in her lesbianism.* It's strange, but in my heart I hear an old hymn we often sang in my little Methodist church:

"Search me, oh God, and know my heart today.

Try me, O Savior. Know my thoughts, I pray.

See if there be some wicked way in me.

Cleanse me from every sin and set me free."

The thought came: *I am caught up again in my own fallen self and groaning on the inside because of the mess I've made of my life.*

There were times when I prayed for Sharon and for our relationship. I <u>did</u> love her—not the way she wanted me to, but like Jonathan and David in the Bible. Is there a godly friendship love two people of the same sex can have? Jack's dad says, Jesus "is a friend that sticketh closer than a brother." I wondered why I had never prayed for God to help me in the relationship between me and my male lover, 'Choir Man'.

Jack was overly curious about the amount of time Sharon and I spent together. He knew we were very close to each other and asked if there was something physical going on between us. My response was to laugh as if the question was ridiculous. "Jack," I would say, "do you actually think Sharon and I are lovers?!" I made it sound as though there was never even a hint of sexuality in my relationship with Sharon—that we had not and were not having sexual contact of any kind. There were long periods of time when Jack wouldn't approach the subject, but then it would begin to eat at him and the questions would come again.

I was such a liar, but it was all part of my way of coping. I would go into denial phase just as I did when I was younger. I had used this technique so many times in my childhood that it was second nature to me and merely another mechanism to help me survive.

The tension between Sharon and me escalated to where we began having heated arguments. "Sharon," I would ask, "what about your church? What about Leonard? What about God?" She always responded with, "You're asking <u>me</u> about <u>my</u> church and <u>my</u> husband? What about yours? What about your big, Calvinistic God who is supposedly working everything out for your good. How is He working for you, for us?" I had no answers for her questions.

Sharon and I crossed boundaries on a regular basis. I enjoyed her tenderness, but she pressured me for more than I was comfortable giving. Friction developed between us as I began to pull away. At times she threatened to tell Jack about our relationship if I ever tried to shut her out of my life.

Over many months, I slowly began to feel trapped. I had 'danced with the devil' and sunk to the level of the unnatural. Most of the time, I felt like nothing more than a lying, cheating, unfaithful, deceitful wretch. How could God <u>not</u> damn my eternal soul? My conversations with Sharon no longer included talk of her wonderful children and husband. She didn't want to talk about them…only us. She seemed driven by a lustful, crazed compulsion—almost verging on demonic, I thought. How quickly sin had turned something as wonderful as a friendship into such a sordid mess!

We both tried to restore our friendship, but the black hole of her emptiness and the perversion of what was needed to fill that black hole were as different as male and female. For over a year I tried to hang on to something I had longed for that just wasn't there—a fulfilling friendship with someone who seemed so right in the beginning. Our moments alone changed from what, at one time, I thought was true friendship to constant sexual advances, followed by apologies and promises that it wouldn't happen again. Finally, I stopped being with Sharon unless Jack, Leonard or their children were around. She continued to threaten she would tell Jack, who was now curious as to why Sharon and I *weren't* spending very much time together. He would ask, "What's happening with you and Sharon? Have you two had a falling out?" "No, Jack, we're both just really busy," I would answer casually. It seemed to satisfy his curiosity. But when he looked at me, I sensed he was thinking there was something more to it than busyness. I lived in fear every day that Sharon would tell Jack of the boundaries we had crossed. Was there ever a day I could remember when I was free from condemnation, guilt, dread and fear of God?

Months passed. The withdrawal from Sharon was slow, heartbreaking and painful. She soon deserted Leonard and the girls, leaving town with another woman who was a known lesbian in our small community. *'Oh, God, please don't give up on me! Don't turn me over to a deceitful and corrupt mind,'* I prayed. Oh, the depth of my depravity! It's no wonder the Bible says the very creation groans under the weight of the curse. I did miss my friend—that's what she really was to me. I prayed for Sharon. Did God hear my prayers? Probably not. Why would He be concerned about me? There was also great relief when Sharon left. Now Jack would never know about the boundaries crossed between the two of us. How wicked and self-serving that thought was!

When Leonard, heartbroken, came over to our house to tell us Sharon had left, Jack and I both tried to comfort him, but it was useless. Through tears, Leonard said he knew Sharon was a lesbian and told us about the many years they had tried to work through the problems it brought to their relationship. He asked several questions about my friendship with Sharon, all resulting in answers from me that were lies. Leonard thanked us for being good, God-fearing neighbors and said he had hoped my Christian friendship with Sharon would have helped her overcome the problem. He said he appreciated all I had done.

After Leonard left, Jack turned, looked directly at me and asked once again if Sharon had ever made physical advances toward me or suggested in any way she wanted to have a sexual relationship with me. I lied again. "Jack," I said, "Sharon confided in me that she was a lesbian and I did my best to help her. We had many talks regarding what the scripture says about unnatural affection. We confided in each other as females will do, but nothing ever happened of a sexual nature." I could see he wasn't buying my story. "Please don't lie to me if something happened," he responded. "We can get past it. I don't want to live under this cloud of suspicion any longer." I didn't like the way he said 'cloud of suspicion'. Did Jack know more than he was saying? "Jack," I said, "<u>nothing happened</u>." "Well, what about all that sanctimonious, legalistic stuff her church preaches?" he asked. Instead of answering him, I responded with a question of my own. "Why is it, Jack, we can claim to be Christians and yet live a life of deceit?" Jack seemed stuck under his 'cloud of suspicion' and didn't answer me. I knew Jack and I had just moved another step further apart because of my lack of truthfulness. Somewhere in the Bible it says a husband does faithfully trust in his wife. Jack couldn't and didn't and I knew it.

There was a period of time after the second abortion and the relationship with Sharon when Jack and I seemed more contented as husband and wife. I often felt the presence of the Lord, but my sinful, deceptive past was always there to eat at me like a cancer. Many times, I wanted to fall into Jack's arms and ask for his forgiveness, but fear would overwhelm me. What if he rejected me? What if he wouldn't forgive me? I kept my secrets and swore I would take them with me to my grave. It felt as if I was in court every day. My conscience accused me, Satan indicted me and for sure God's strict justice and holy law made me fearful. And, yes, Jack's 'cloud of suspicion' was still there hanging heavy over our relationship.

A couple of years after the affair with 'Choir Man', I found myself pregnant again. Jack and I were going to have our first child. I gave birth to an eight-pound, two-ounce boy—our Jacob Elect. He was a precious little bundle of joy. I marveled at him and was in awe at how he was Jack and me wrapped up in one flesh.

Jacob inherited traits from both of us. He showed early signs of being athletic like his father and I just knew he would play football someday. He was a lover and it wasn't long before he had his mother wrapped around his little finger. But Jacob grew fast and it didn't take me long to realize he had my nature. Our Jacob was precious, but he was a deceptive child and it showed itself early in him.

My own experiences had certainly led me to believe what my father-in-law calls the 'T' in 'Tulip': total depravity. I saw it first in myself, then in my son. I thought about the scripture that says we come out of our mother's womb speaking lies. Is an infant depraved at birth? If babies are born liars, how can infants who die go to heaven? Did I eternally damn my two infants by aborting them?! They had no opportunity to believe. Jack's dad teaches that salvation is not by chance. It is the plan of a sovereign God through the doing and dying of His Son. In the Bible, when King David's baby boy died, he said, "But now he is dead…can I bring him back again? I shall go to him…" Maybe I, too, will get to see my babies. Oh, dear God, what have I done?! The 'Tulip' people believe babies are sinners even before they show it through overt actions. Jack's dad doesn't sprinkle babies, because he says no holy water can wash them clean of their sin nature. How could my precious babies be haters of God? But, then, they came out of me and my own wicked transgressions testify against me. How could my birth children not have my sinful nature? What a mess!

Even in the church there seems to be no demonstration of a dying of the old man and a powerful new creation that loves holiness. Look at me and 'Choir Man'. He's married. I'm married. I'm a deacon's daughter! Then there's my dad—the deacon pedophile! There just can't be any hope in humanity! Can there be hope <u>for</u> humanity? I suppose there can be if there truly is a God who is mighty enough and gracious enough to do for man what man cannot do for himself. I wonder if that makes me a 'Tulip' person. They certainly believe in a God who is sovereign, gracious and powerful. My dad used to tell me Jack's 'Tulip' Baptist church believed all babies went to hell. Then again, he was the same man who started raping me at ten years of age and continued to do so repeatedly during my teen years! I would hate to think hell is filled with babies and a pedophile—that those innocent little ones could be in the same place with my perverted, deacon father!

Thinking about my dad and the church where I grew up made me remember there were some real saints who attended there. My childhood Sunday School teacher, Maw Nanny, made the Bible come alive for me. During those awful years of molestation, precious 'Mother in Israel', as Pastor Johnson called her, was always there with an encouraging lesson. It was from her tender, loving lips I first felt and sensed there was hope for my ugliness in the love and grace of God. Maw Nanny was the kindest, most nurturing woman I've ever known and seemed to sense my need for mothering care. How strange, since she had no idea what my father was doing to me…nor did any of the rest of the membership of that little congregation.

My mother was into her own wants and needs. She was a broken woman, verbally abused and neglected by my father. She surely knew what happened almost every Saturday morning in my bedroom. She knew he was in there with me. I could tell by the way she looked at me she was aware of what he was doing. It was almost like her eyes were apologizing and at the same time filled with anger toward me. What kind of mother doesn't protect her daughter from the sexual advances of a father? But, then I must ask myself: What kind of mother has her babies suctioned from her womb? Maybe a mother who comes into the world with a sin nature? Who am I to judge my own mother? Are we all animals? How can we do these things and have any hope of Heaven? Is there a Heaven? How can I ever be right with God? I have so many questions! If God is just, I don't see how there can be any hope for me. Thank you, Maw Nanny, for the things you gave to me in my childhood. You gave me hope for change, hope of a new birth, a new creation, hope of being right with God. You were a beacon in my wilderness. Many things were so fuzzy when it came to being right with God, but sometimes there was a beam of light that shone in my dark cellar…moments when I thought I actually <u>could</u> be a child of God.

Jack knew things weren't right between us and asked on several occasions if there was anything we needed to talk about. Once, he went a step further and wanted to know if there was someone else. He must have known, or at least suspected, I'd had an affair, as he knew I wasn't single minded toward him. His heart couldn't safely trust in me. Jack became more attentive and I think he tried to fill my emptiness, but it just wasn't enough. I continued to walk through life feeling like there was more, that there was someone else for me. At the same time, I felt tremendous condemnation toward myself for my lack of love and faithfulness to my husband.

Two years after Jacob was born, our second child, Isaac Elect, came into the world. Motherhood was draining for me, plus I had feelings of guilt for wishing I wasn't pregnant while carrying Isaac—it had cramped my lifestyle. Doubts and old temptations had haunted me. Abortion crossed my mind again. Oh, I know my feelings were self-centered. Nonetheless, abortion weighed heavily on my mind during those months. I have asked God to forgive me many times for even thinking about aborting Isaac. He is such a tender child and I am sure God is going to use him in His ministry.

Life went on and the years passed quickly. Jack's business continued to grow and the boys grew as well, becoming little men, 10 and 12 years old. As for me, at just 36 I felt like I'd missed life. The years brought good and bad times, but the black hole in me was ever present. I attended church with Jack and the boys and came to see and believe that salvation is of the Lord. I realize salvation is composed of grace, but I often wondered if even unmerited favor is enough for God to reach me.

There were two points Jack's dad preached over the years that always thrilled me and gave me a sense of wonderment. The first was: God's love for us is without a cause. We have done nothing to deserve his love and can do nothing to earn it. The second point was: If it is without a cause, if it's free, then this free love opens the door to an adulterer like me. I'm horrified at my own depravity! How can a holy God love a wretch like me? It must be because He loves me 'freely'! I wonder if that makes me a 'Tulip' person.

I went back to college, but the restlessness within was constantly chipping away at me. I seemed to still be searching for something or someone to fill the black hole in my life. This time around, most of the students in my classes were much younger than I. Almost immediately, a very nice gentleman caught my attention. Actually, he was one of my professors. He was kind to me, attentive and always very interested in what I had to say. He was a sharp dresser and very pleasing to the eye, except for a rather large scar on the side of his head. I never asked about it, though, as I thought a question like that was much too personal. Thinking about it now, I realize, after a while I didn't even notice it anymore. It's funny how time does things like that.

Professor Luci's class was dealing with how all things are relative. He didn't believe in absolutes. I never asked him, but I often thought: *How can you believe <u>absolutely</u> there are no absolutes?* He would say, "There is no good or no evil. There is just substance. Who can really say there is evil in the world? The idea that there is some demonic spirit called the 'Devil' or 'Satan', who rebelled against The Creator Spirit and was cast out of Utopia, is hardly believable to the intelligent mind. Look deep within yourselves and you will discover a much higher animal than the one presented in guilt-ridden religious philosophy."

I admit Professor Luci fascinated me. The attraction was strong and I started 'accidently' running into him after class—which soon led to lunch invitations and chit-chat. He was such a good listener and seemed to hang on my every word. It wasn't long before I found myself telling him about my marriage, complaining about all of Jack's bad traits in the process but purposely leaving out how wonderful he was in other areas. Professor Luci seemed to understand Jack just wasn't giving me what I needed. I became aware of a certain amount of relief I felt inside when I pointed out Jack's flaws and quickly realized it was because doing that made me focus less on my own. The professor talked about his wife and frequently slipped into the conversation how self-centered she was. Once, when I asked to see a picture of her, he said he didn't carry one. (I remember thinking how curious it was that he had no pictures of her and didn't wear a wedding band either.) It wasn't long before we each had quite a case built against our spouses.

I soon realized I was in way over my head...again! Things got out of hand quickly and I found myself in the middle of another affair. Almost before I knew it, the professor was begging me to leave Jack and come live with him. I guess it never crossed my mind to ask how that would be possible. What about his wife? Where would she go? He told me he was wealthy and could supply my every material need. I was caught like the proverbial fly in a spider's web, but couldn't bring myself to take that final step. I just couldn't leave Jack…yet.

Every day was a good day. I was happy most of the time, except for the pangs of guilt and condemnation that occasionally stabbed me in my heart of hearts. The truth was, I looked forward to sending the boys off to school and Jack to work so I could anxiously await my mid-morning call from Professor Luci.

Unfortunately, Jack wasn't feeling well one morning and was still in the house when the call came. "I'll get it," I yelled and quickly grabbed the phone. It was too late. Jack had already picked up the extension only to hear Professor Luci recite his daily greeting of "You are so beautiful and I especially loved the way you looked yesterday." I had to think quickly! "I'm sorry. This is the Elect household. You must have the wrong number. Goodbye," I said politely.

I hurriedly hung up the phone, planning to call Professor Luci later in the morning to explain what had happened. Jack hung up the extension and left for work without saying a word to me. Did he know? I comforted myself with a recent news article I had read, which stated that approximately 89% of husbands whose wives commit adultery never find out about the affair. I felt sure my lies had sufficiently covered my tracks—or at least I hoped so.

Even though I was having another affair, I kept up the façade of my church life, which continued to be part of our family routine. Often, while sitting in God's house, I reached a point of almost vomiting because of the awful pangs of condemnation I was feeling inside. One Sunday, I felt particularly nauseated hearing the pastor preach from Romans 7, where the Apostle Paul says what he wanted to do he didn't, and what he hated was what he did! In this passage Paul is confessing the wretchedness of his flesh and his desire to be delivered from this body of death. Jack's dad said Paul had been preaching for almost 30 years when he made this statement. *Could there be hope for me?* After thirty years of preaching, the Apostle Paul himself still cried out, "Oh, wretched man THAT I AM!" Pastor moved from Romans 7 and ended his sermon with Romans 8:1, "There is therefore NOW NO CONDEMNATION TO THEM WHICH ARE IN CHRIST JESUS..." *I surely am not in Christ Jesus. How can I be? I am an adulteress!* In spite of my sin, though, in spite of my wickedness, there was a sense that this God of grace is a greater Savior than I was a sinner. *Can there be hope for me? Maybe.*

How had I reached this awful place in my life? I must stop—for my sake, for my children's sake, for my husband's sake, but most of all, for the glory of my Savior who loves me and gave Himself for me.

When I was overwhelmed by the love of God, I would tell myself the affair <u>had</u> to be over. I did this often; but, then, fear would creep in and I wondered how I could ever tell Jack. What would he do? What effect would it have on my boys, my church, my in-laws? Maybe I could just stop the affair and take another dirty secret with me to the grave. This reasoning always brought me some measure of peace, but only temporarily. My secret held me in bondage to my lover. To be free, I would have to confess to Jack as I had to my Lord. That 'cloud of suspicion' had never left and still hovered over him every day. It manifested itself in his countenance and in our conversation. There was no way I could tell him the truth.

Days, weeks, months passed. Could it really be a year since I began this affair with Professor Luci? Every day we talked and laughed, had lunch, then ended our time together in bed. He constantly repeated his request, asking me to leave Jack and be with him. He was so convincing when he said my children were young and would recover from the divorce. I knew I was dangerously close to surrendering to his proposition.

Despite what was going in my secret life, there were times at home when I felt close to Jack and so in love with him…almost like the sense of excitement I had when we were first dating. He was a good man, a constant provider, a wonderful father and he really was a loving husband. Me? I was nothing short of disgusting! The tug-of-war taking place inside me was unbearable. *Maybe I can tell him the truth. He is a good man. He might forgive me. Oh, what am I talking about?! It's much too late! There's no turning back! I can't bear his kind words any longer! His kindness only serves as a reminder to me of my wretchedness! The internal torture I have is eating me alive! I'm finished with it all! It's over!* I made the decision to leave Jack and be with Luci.

When I told Luci my marriage was over and I wanted to be with him, he was ecstatic. We began to finalize our plan for the escape we had talked about so often. I would leave Jack and Luci would leave his wife on the same day. Getting everything over with quickly was the best way to handle this. Dragging the issue out would serve no purpose for anyone involved. Jack deserved someone more worthy—someone who would love him and be the wife he needed. I was confident that once the divorce was settled I would be able to see my boys on a regular basis. Luci had money, which meant I could spoil my sons with gifts and opportunities they would otherwise not have had…and Jack would be free to find the wife he deserved. Yes, this would work. In the long run, I was convinced it would be better for everyone.

Luci and I planned to fly to Europe and stay there until the initial shock wore off. I would leave the boys a note explaining why I had to leave, but that I loved them very much. I wrote a separate note to Jack telling him what an awful person I was and how he deserved so much more than I could give him. The thought crossed my mind that it was rather strange, even wicked, that I never considered Luci's wife's feelings. What would she think? What would happen to her?

The day we had decided upon arrived. As I sat on the swing and basked in the bright sunlight shining on the familiar surroundings of my front yard, a stretch limousine pulled up in front of our house. *He is certainly doing this thing right!* Luci waited in the car and reached out his hand to me as the chauffeur opened the door. I took hold of his hand and stepped into the back seat…into my new life.

The ride to the airport wasn't going to be a long one. In the meantime there was expensive champagne to drink and hors d'ouvres to munch on. We held hands, snuggled close to each other and kissed passionately, feeling the excitement of our pending 'honeymoon'. There was such an extremely highly-charged sexual atmosphere in the back seat of the limousine I didn't know if we would be able to restrain ourselves physically. Luci seemed almost out of his mind with euphoria. Everything felt wonderful to me, too!

So many thoughts were racing through my mind all at once—some that began to cloud the excitement of the moment. *I am now with someone who is not a Christian, not a believer and shows very little interest in anything related to God. Strange I should have such a thought, for am I truly a Christian? How could I be? Surely, I'm not. If so, I am under the awful condemnation of a holy God!* The worry and doubt that had plagued me most of my life came to the forefront of my mind again. *Enough of these thoughts! I just need to be in this moment and bathe myself in the enjoyment of it all!*

Still, Jack came to my mind. *He won't be home for another two hours and the boys are spending the night at his parents' house. By the time he reads my letter, Luci and I will be high over the ocean in his private jet. How is he going to handle all of this? It doesn't matter! I won't have to deal with any of the heated emotions brought on by what I've done. I'll be enjoying Paris with the man I love and who loves me! Right?*

When we reached the airport, we entered through a private gate and rode a short distance to a hanger containing several private jets. The security personnel at the gate addressed Luci with lots of "Sirs" and "Yes, sirs". The two of us walked to the plane, where we were greeted by the pilot, co-pilot and two flight attendants, who would be at our beck and call for the trip to Paris.

Stepping inside the plane, I was overwhelmed by the luxury I saw before me...accoutrements that were mind-boggling to a small town girl. There was a dining area, a bedroom with a large screen for watching movies and a study equipped with an executive desk, a white leather chair, two couches, a computer and a telephone. What more could I want? Peace of mind, perhaps.

As the jet took to the skies, I flinched from a pain that reached deep into the pit of my stomach. *What have I done?* Seeing that I looked a bit nervous, Luci instructed one of the flight attendants to bring me a drink. The liquor felt good going down and immediately began to calm the anxiety I was experiencing. By the time the plane reached its cruising altitude, I had consumed enough alcohol to leave me feeling blissfully relaxed. Between the quiet hum of the engines and the drinks, I was soon lulled into a deep sleep.

The End of Life

When I awoke, we were at least two hours into our nine-hour flight. I slowly opened my eyes to see Luci and his two flight attendants standing over me...grinning. One of the flight attendants asked me if I had enjoyed my last sleeping moments on earth.

"What? What do you mean?" I asked, confused and somewhat frightened by his tone and the demonic look in his eyes.

Luci spoke with a voice I'd never heard from him...or anyone else I'd ever known. "Foreknown, you stupid little bitch! You are as gullible as your ancestor, Eve. Don't you know who I am?" The tenderness I had always seen in his eyes was gone. There was nothing left but a piercing, wicked emptiness. Then, I saw it—the scar on his head that was so prominent when we first met, but faded as our relationship progressed. It was more hideous than I remembered and seemed to fit with the ominous face now staring through the very soul of me. My fear began to take on a life of its own as it rose to a level I'd never experienced! *What's happening?! Who is this?! Am I still asleep and having a nightmare?!*

The stench of his breath was indescribable as he moved closer to my face and spoke again in that horrible voice. "What in your ignorant little mind made you think a college professor could afford a private jet? You never questioned any of the lies I told you, and you certainly never dreamed I was Luci…fer, the Pharmacia ruler of the world, did you?! I have had my eye on you since the day you were born. I knew you were a weak vessel and that I could have you. My design from the beginning has been to damn you to the lowest hell. Your own 'religious' father was one of my messengers, but you were too stupid to figure that out—and even more stupid to not see through Sharon, your girlfriend! Remember? You liked her, didn't you? You <u>loved</u> her, didn't you? And, of course, you <u>do</u> remember Mr. 'Choir Man'. Ah, yes, there was also my dear friend, Dr. Slaughter. You certainly used his services a lot in your ignorant attempt to cover the fact that you are nothing more than a common, street whore!

"Oh, for some reason, you have been a tough one, Foreknown—always reaching out to your God for grace and mercy. Now, you are finally in my clutches! Is there anything else you would like before my assistants and I exit the plane? Perhaps a little something to sedate the reality of what is about to happen? You, my little, deceived Foreknown, are going to die—after that, the second death! Then you are mine for all eternity!"

This was no dream! It was really happening! Oh, the fear and shame that gripped my soul! I was over the middle of the ocean with evil incarnate…Lucifer and four of his demons! Out of the six of us, I was the only one who was going to die tonight! I knew Lucifer and his hoards couldn't die! Spirits can only be controlled by the ONE greater than they!

"Oh, God," I cried, "please forgive me! Jack, I've been a fool! Precious boys, look to Jesus!"

Lucifer and his friends laughed and mocked me as I called on the Lord. I felt once again like that dirty, pitiful, abused, used, little girl. *Oh, Lord, am I on my way to hell?!*

In the blink of an eye, I was the only one left—the other five had disappeared! The realization that I was inside a plane at 30,000 feet with no pilot hit me like a kick in the stomach! Overcome with mind-numbing fear, I jumped up and ran to the cockpit. The plane appeared to be set on automatic pilot and flying on its own, but the fuel needle told me the tank was empty. I knew it was just one more thing Lucifer had done to increase the torture of my dying moments. There was not enough time to radio for help—alarms were blaring, confirming that the jet was out of fuel. Gasping engines caused the plane to shudder with a violent force, as the nose began to tip downward. I knew I only had seconds until the plane hit the water. Turning, I saw the exit door and made an instant decision. I was going to die, but I wasn't going to step into eternity and meet my

Maker from Satan's plane! Using every ounce of strength within me, I forced the door open and jumped!

My life on earth flashed before me like a movie stuck on fast forward. I saw my sexually-abusive father, then my sweet, loving husband, Jack, who I betrayed. I saw my sons, Jacob and Isaac, to whom I never portrayed the characteristics of the virtuous woman of Proverbs 31. I saw the adulterous "Choir Man", Luci…fer with his demons and my other immoral lover. Then I saw the 'little ones' I had aborted. *Oh, dear God, what is happening?! My thoughts are racing! I must be about to stand before God in judgment!*

At the moment of my death, there was one passage of scripture that flashed through my mind. It contained the words of Job: "For I know that my Redeemer liveth…and though after my skin worms destroy this body, yet in my flesh shall I see God…"

BREAKING NEWS

"A small plane was reportedly seen plunging into the Atlantic Ocean approximately two hours flight time from the east coast of the United States. Details are sketchy at this time. More information will be reported as it becomes available."

SUDDENLY, I AM AWARE OF MY SURROUNDINGS. MY PHYSICAL PAIN IS TREMENDOUS AND I'M BARELY CONSCIOUS. THE TASTE OF LIQUOR IS STILL ON MY BREATH

AND I'M DRENCHED WITH A MIX OF SEA WATER AND JET FUEL. WHERE AM I? AM I ALIVE? AM I DEAD? TOTAL CONFUSION! WHERE IS LUCI? NO! I DON'T WANT TO SEE LUCI! I KNOW WHO HE IS AND HE INTENDS TO DAMN ME!!!

Two days later, a small article in the newspaper read:

PRIVATE JET PLUNGES INTO ATLANTIC OCEAN

"Passengers, enjoying their last few days of a trans-Atlantic cruise, watched in horror as a small, private jet plunged into the cold waters of the Atlantic Ocean approximately three miles off the starboard side of the ship. The captain of the 'Indulgence', one of five mega-ships owned and operated by 'Worldly Pleasures Cruise Line', reportedly instructed his crew to increase the ship's speed in order to reach the location more quickly, as a number of passengers thought they had seen something fall from the plane moments before it entered the water.

Upon arriving in the vicinity of the downed plane, the ship's crew recovered the lifeless body of a young female, approximately 35-40 years of age, found floating in the water. The body, badly bruised and broken, was retrieved and brought onboard the 'Indulgence'. The woman could not be immediately identified, as she had no documents on her person. Nothing more was recovered, including no other bodies. The captain commented he thought it was quite peculiar that no debris from the plane could be seen floating anywhere in the area.

The FAA is reporting that all aircraft have been accounted for with the exception of a small, private jet bound for Paris, France, which left an unnamed airport approximately two hours before the aforementioned plane went down. This private jet is assumed to be the same plane that plunged into the Atlantic. The roster filed at the airport listed those on board as: a pilot, a co-pilot, two flight attendants, a Mr. Luci, owner of the plane, and a female passenger, Foreknown Elect. A reliable source has informed this paper that no relatives could be found for anyone on board other than Ms. Elect. Her family was notified of the accident and will be asked to identify the body as soon as it is available. The FAA is promising to launch a full investigation and will be forthcoming with further information at a later date."

Wait! Now, what's happening? I feel myself being transported back to earth, to a beautiful white building—a funeral home! I see my mortal body lying there in a casket. I am amazed! It was so badly broken from the impact with the ocean I wouldn't have believed there was anything to recover. Only God's mercy could have made that possible for the sake of my loved ones. Oh, Jack, I see you here, too, in this private room—just you and my spiritless, lifeless body. You move your chair close to my casket so you can touch me, kiss me, hold my cold hand and speak softly to me. Why am I here? Why do I have to listen to the husband I loved, yet was so unfaithful to? What, Jack? You're apologizing for failing as a husband? You knew about things I was doing, but were afraid you would lose me if you confronted me? You think you are weak? Oh, yes, Jack, I saw that horrible 'cloud of suspicion' in your face and I saw your fear. It was there every day. I knew it and that you were trying to cope, but couldn't. I knew you wanted me to reach out to you in truthfulness and confession. I know now you would have forgiven me. Oh, Jack, if I had only told you how confused I was. I wish I had confessed and sought help for the abuse at my 'religious' father's hands. I wish I had never known another man or woman. How could I have done this to you and the boys? Oh, my sweet sons. Are they OK? They're heartbroken? You don't know how they will ever recover? Jack, I can't bear to hear that. The burden is too great! How I wish you could hear me. Soon I will stand before Almighty God in judgment! I deserve His holy and awful condemnation for what I am and for what I've done! If you could only hear me, if you could only know how dirty I feel and how sorry I am for the life I lived!

Someone's at the door. It's the funeral director. Jack, wait! I want to talk more! No, don't leave, Jack, please! Where are they taking my body, Jack? Are you coming? Jack, please don't leave me alone! I want to tell you about Professor Luci and what happened! Jack, it was all a set up! Satan desired me and there were five others on the plane with me—all demons! Jack, they left me on the plane alone! Please don't leave, Jack! I'm so frightened!

I watch my mortal body as it is pushed down the hall into a large room filled with beautiful flowers and sad, confused mourners. I immediately see my first lover, who is there with his wife and children. Wasn't he a demon like the others? Oh, God of Heaven, how wicked and hurtful the nature of fallen men and women! As I look over the crowd, I see so many friends from our church. Jack's mom and dad are here. Will he conduct my funeral? And there...my precious little boys, Isaac and Jacob. Please, don't cry, sweet sons. I am here and I love you. I'm so sorry! Oh, if I could only hold them once more.

The music is beginning. I always loved, 'It Is Well with My Soul'. Did Jack remember? Yes, yes, that's what they're singing. How thrilling to hear it even at this late hour!

> "My sin, oh, the bliss of this glorious thought!
> My sin, not in part but the whole,
> Is nailed to the cross and I bear it no more,
> Praise the Lord, praise the Lord, O my soul."

Thank you, Jack, for having them sing this song. I know you will remember the second one, as well. We talked about my two favorite hymns so many times. They're your favorites as well, aren't they, Jack? You and I even sang them together. Oh, the comfort I felt from their message! Thank you, Jack, for remembering. They're beginning to sing 'How Great Thou Art'.

71

"And when I think, that God, His son not sparing;

Sent Him to die, I scarce can take it in;

That on the cross, my burden gladly bearing,

He bled and died to take away my sin.

Then sings my soul, my Savior God, to Thee,

How great Thou art, how great Thou art."

I'm so glad for the times you and I were able to talk about the Savior, Jack. Your dad always comforted me with his messages of the marvelous grace of God. I never felt he preached like some say the Calvinists preach, "Shall we continue in sin, that grace may abound?" In fact, I realize the more he preached the grace of this amazing God, the more I hated my evil ways.

Jack's dad is standing and about to speak. I wonder what he will say about me now—he must be so angry. I have deserted his son, his grandsons and brought such shame on his ministry. There can be nothing good for him to say.

Jack's dad begins to speak to the mourners. "If you have your Bible with you, please turn to the 8th chapter of the book of Romans. I will read only the first verse. 'There is therefore now no condemnation to them which are in Christ Jesus, who walk not after the flesh, but after the spirit.'"

I have never listened to the Word with more intensity than today. It's as if I have ears to hear! I have such a hunger and thirst to hear a word from the Lord!

Jack's father continues. "We are all here today with broken hearts. Confusion and fear are present with us. We are aware of the sinful acts and events that led to Foreknown's tragic death and there is no one here today who doesn't have questions about where she is at this moment. There's a deep searching in our souls causing all of us to cry out, 'Search <u>me</u>, O God, and know <u>my</u> heart today. Try <u>me</u>, O Savior, know <u>my</u> thoughts, I pray. See if there be some wicked way in <u>me</u>. Cleanse <u>me</u> from every sin and set <u>me</u> free'. May God comfort you today with the gospel of the glory of the Lord. Foreknown Elect, if you can hear me, may God give you HOPE in the Lord Jesus Christ.

"The Apostle in Romans, chapter 7, struggled against inward sin and, at the same time, rejoiced in complete justification. Paul said, 'So then with the mind I myself serve the law of God; but with the flesh the law of sin.' He goes on to say, 'THERE IS THEREFORE NOW NO CONDEMNATION...'! What is the message here? It simply means believers are in a state of conflict, but not in a state of condemnation. When the conflicts and struggles of life are at their peak, the believer is still JUSTIFIED. When the believer has to do his utmost just to stand his ground, when he feels he cannot advance an inch without fighting for it, when he cries out in agony because of vehement temptation, 'O wretched man that I am', he can still place his hand on the word of God and say, 'and yet there is no condemnation towards me, for I am in Christ Jesus.'

"It is this experience which puzzles the very people who are benefactors of His free justification. I am sure Foreknown, like all of us if we are honest, struggled with this very issue. If Foreknown belonged to the Lord when she boarded that corporate jet, there was a struggle going on in her soul. With all my watching and warring, with all my fears and trembling; yet will I rejoice in the Lord even now; for 'There is therefore now no condemnation to them which are in Christ Jesus…'!

"It is the great and merciful design of the gospel to acquaint chosen, elect sinners, who were guilty and condemned by the Holy Law of God and given over to justice to carry out the sentence of condemnation, as to how they will be pardoned and justified.

"The chosen sinner cannot be happy until he has some evidence of being pardoned and made righteous, and it is the gospel alone, in the power of the Holy Spirit, that tells him of his pardon and justification. Thus, he has peace with God.

"The gospel must be confirmed constantly, for it would seem that chosen sinners, because of their internal struggle with sin and outward circumstances, do continually doubt their acquittal. I am sure Foreknown often fought this battle, as do I and every little child of God. Foreknown, I hope you can hear me today!

"The terror of condemnation is unspeakable. When we come to an understanding of what condemnation implies and learn it's meaning, we plead like David, '…enter not into judgment with thy servant'. 'Condemnation' means: a sentence pronounced with a suggestion of the punishment following. It indicates a decision has been reached as the result of an investigation and now sentencing is expected. It is the process of judgment, which ultimately leads to a decision, which entails a sentence based on one's faults, as the result of an investigation. So then, 'condemnation' is the sentence dooming an individual to everlasting punishment as a result of an investigation by the law. The sentence, therefore, must be carried out according to justice.

"The investigation which leads to condemnation will bring the guilty to a final separation from the God who made us. It means some will see the face of God no more and will be eternally cut off from all hope of salvation. There will be no more invitations to come to Christ, all you who are burdened and heavy laden, so He can give you rest; no more singing of 'Just as I am, without one plea, but that Thy blood was shed for me…Oh, Lamb of God, I come'.

" 'Condemnation' brings separation from the precious Redeemer, who was slighted, despised and rejected of men. It means separation from the Holy Spirit, the Comforter, who did strive for men and women to come to Christ. 'Condemnation' means to be cast into everlasting fire, thrown into that black hole of outer, bottomless darkness. 'Condemnation' means one's eternal companions will be Satan, his angels and depraved men and women who shall be weeping and wailing and gnashing their teeth in the lust of unfulfilled desire. 'Condemnation' means God's law is against one, and that one will receive the damnatory sentence of the law.

"There comes a day of judgment. He has appointed a day in which he will 'judge the world in righteousness'. 'And it is appointed unto men once to die, but after this the judgment.' He shall come 'in flaming fire taking vengeance on them that know not God, and that obey not the gospel'.

"Oh, how I thank God for the gospel, the power of God unto salvation. What a dilemma old King Darius must have faced when Daniel, his friend, was thrown into the lions' den for breaking the law. He paced the floor all night long, trying to find a way to be just <u>and</u> justifier of Daniel, but he could not do it. The dilemma of King Darius is the glory of God. He has found a way to be just <u>and</u> justifier of the ungodly. 'Bless the LORD, O my soul: and all that is within me, bless his holy name.' He has found a way to go down into the coal mine of sin but not become Himself dirty. He, Himself, found a way to drink my damnation dry, to remove my sins 'as far as the east is from the west'. He has found a way whereby He can say, 'It is finished', it is accomplished and it is done.

"Oh, when He had by Himself purged our sins, He sat down to the right of God, waiting for His enemies and mine to become His footstool. Immanuel, God in human flesh, stepped out of eternity into mortal time and came here, not to spy out our sins, but to deliver us <u>from</u> our sins. He, Himself, being the ram caught in the thicket; He, Himself, being JEHOVAH-JIREH (the Lord will provide), came to die for us. He is the Lamb of God. He is the Sacrifice. He is the Mercy Seat. He is the Propitiation. He is the Door. He is the Way. He is the Truth. He is Wonderful, Counselor, Mighty God, Everlasting Father, Prince of Peace, Rose of Sharon, Lily of the Valley, Bright and Morning Star, Fairest of Ten Thousand. He is the Resurrection and the Life. He is the Living Vine. He is the Door to Heaven. He is the Bread of Life. He is the Water of Life. He is the Author and Finisher of our Faith. He is Peacemaker. He is Advocate and Intercessor.

"Since there is 'NO CONDEMNATION' to those who are in Christ Jesus, then we may rest assured that 'Blessed are the dead who die in the Lord.'

" 'I won't have to cross Jordan alone. Jesus died all my sins to atone. When the darkness I see, He'll be waiting for me. I won't have to cross Jordan alone.'

"He did intimately love us, predestinate us, call us, justify us and will He not surely glorify us?! Foreknown, can you hear me? Foreknown, shout when you stand before Him, 'unto Him that loved me and loosed me from my sins in His own blood'!

"Sing, Foreknown! Sing before Him and make a joyful noise! 'Sing the wondrous love of Jesus; sing His mercy and His grace. In the mansions bright and blessed' He's 'prepared for us a place. When we all get to heaven, what a day of rejoicing that will be! When we all see Jesus, we'll sing and shout the victory! While we walk the pilgrim pathway, clouds will overspread the sky; but when traveling days are over, not a shadow, not a sigh.'

"Now, dear family and friends, I end this service today by reading to you again from Romans 8, but this time we will leave the first verse and catch up with Paul as he closes the chapter, beginning with verse 28 and reading through verse 39.

" 'And we know that all things work together for good to them that love God, to them who are called according to his purpose. For whom he did foreknow, he also did predestinate to be conformed to the image of his Son, that he might be the firstborn among many brethren. Moreover whom he did predestinate, them he also called; and whom he called, them he also justified; and whom he justified, them he also glorified. What shall we then say to these things? If God be for us, who can be against us? He that spared not his own son, but delivered him up for us all, how shall he not with him also freely give us all things? Who shall lay any thing to the charge of God's elect? It is God that justifieth. Who is he that CONDEMNETH? It is Christ that died, yea rather, that is risen again, who is even at the right hand of God, who also maketh intercession for us. Who shall separate us from the love of Christ? Shall tribulation, or distress, or persecution, or famine, or nakedness, or peril, or sword? As it is written, For thy sake we are killed all the day long; we are accounted as sheep for the slaughter. Nay, in all these things we are more than conquerors through him that loved us. For I am persuaded, that neither death, nor life, nor angels, nor principalities, nor powers, nor things present, nor things to come, nor height, nor depth, nor any other creature, shall be able to separate us from the love of God, which is in Christ Jesus our Lord.' "

My father-in-law ends with these wonderful verses from God's Word. What a comfort it is to hear him preach one more time. Oh, I do pray that the gospel of free grace is true. Without it there is no hope for me.

Jack's dad looks so tired. Everyone does. I've created such a horrible mess for the ones who loved me the most.

The funeral director steps forward and speaks. "This concludes the funeral service for Foreknown Elect. Friends and family may pass by the casket one last time. If you would then please go to your cars, we will proceed to the cemetery for burial."

So many walk past my casket—godly women from my life who I would never have thought were experiencing spiritual struggles. They surprise me with their secret battles of the flesh. They whisper in my mortal ear and give accounts of how they have hurt like me— how they have struggled with issues of acceptance. They speak of the empty-hole vacuum that sucks at their soul.

Oh, there's Maw Nanny, my precious Sunday School teacher. I can't believe what she's saying to me!

"Oh, Foreknown, I knew you were hurting as a little girl. I suspected your father might have been inappropriate with you and I want you to know it wasn't your fault. You were a victim. I don't know if your mother ever told you I spoke with her. She seemed fearful and wouldn't talk to me about what she called 'a private matter'. Dear child, I fully expect to see you in that city not built with human hands. You will be safe and protected there. I promise I will talk with Jack often and try to be a comfort to him as he struggles through the weeks and months ahead. I will visit with Jacob and Isaac and tell them what a wonderful little girl their mother was."

She's hesitating over my casket. What is it? I'm sensing she feels like she failed me. Oh, 'Mother in Israel', you <u>never</u> failed me! You were kind and loving to me at a time in my life when I was so needy and vulnerable. Thank you for all you taught me. She pats my face with her time-worn hands and walks away, weeping.

I wish Maw Nanny had come after 'Choir Man'. Her words were so encouraging, but His words sting. He has the same look in his eyes he had that Sunday morning when Jack's dad told the story of Hosea and Gomer and the same look as the demons on the plane!

"So, little Miss Foreknown, how naive you were to think demons don't sing in the church choir. As you can now see, they do! It's all just part of the plan. I'm sure I'll be seeing you soon."

'Choir Man's' wife comes next with her children following her. She bends over my casket as if she is going to speak words of comfort or maybe forgiveness, but she doesn't.

"You were not the only woman in the world to search out sexual experiences with other men besides your husband to fill the emptiness in your heart. Oh, I know all about what you told my husband—that Jack was never home, that you wanted to be loved, that you wanted him to compliment you. You wanted! You wanted! Well,

'Choir Man' gave you <u>all</u> of your 'wants', didn't he? Then, you dropped him and kept on searching. Guess you were following the part in your Holy Book that says something about seek and you will find. Just how did it turn out with you and Professor Luci?" *Her sarcasm is repulsively sadistic!* "One more thing I want you to know. Every time 'Choir Man' came home from being with you, the two of us stayed up and laughed about your messed up life. Then we'd have sex with each other. You never suspected demons go to church, did you? Well, I, too, was part of the plan."

As she and her children walk away from my casket, the expression on her face exposes her for what she is—a demon with a sense of accomplishment for the misery she has caused, yet filled with anger for the eternal damnation she faces.

Who are the women standing here now? It's Sharon! She's come with her friend and they both have that look which has now become so familiar to me—the look of the 'evil one'! She leans over the casket and speaks to me.

"You little religious hypocrite! How STUPID you were to feel comfort from my sexual advances! Did you actually think I could love you or any other female in that unnatural way? Love and comfort are foreign to me—I know nothing of them. Loving you was never my goal. Deceiving you was my goal! Clearly, my part in the plan worked. I hope you rot in hell!" *Oh, dear God, have mercy on me!*

Everyone is finally gone from the room except for family. My parents are walking toward the casket to say goodbye for the last time. Oh, no! My dad's face has the same look I saw on the faces of those on the plane, on "Choir Man' and his wife, on Sharon and her friend! He says nothing to me. There is nothing to say. His eyes narrow as he gives me a devilish, smirking glance and walks away. Even now, I shudder to think of what he did to me—especially now, since I know who he really is!

My dear, broken mother falls onto the casket, sobbing, speaking in a hushed voice no one else hears.

"Oh, Foreknown, I'm so sorry. I knew what was happening and did nothing. I was frightened and angry and ashamed something so horrible was going on in our home. I blamed you—it was easier than confronting your dad with the terrible things he was doing. I made myself believe you were enticing him and he couldn't help himself. The time I cut your hair was to make you ugly so he wouldn't want you anymore. How could I have blamed my sweet, innocent child for such unspeakable deeds? How could I have looked the other way? I should have protected you, no matter what. I beg you, forgive me for not being the mother you so desperately needed." *Oh, mother! Please hear me! There is no more anger in my heart toward anyone. Please don't cry! I do forgive you!*

The Funeral Director comes and gently lifts my poor mother off my dead body. Her legs are so weak he is all but carrying her to the lobby of the funeral home.

My in-laws are standing off to the side with Jack and my precious sons, Isaac and Jacob. Jack's parents were always so good to me. They treated me like a daughter and I've totally disappointed them. I know they're absolutely devastated by what I've done to their son and grandsons. They're both weeping as they come to the side of the casket. Jack's mother is speaking softly.

"Foreknown, we love you and always have. We know you would want us to help take care of the boys. We will be there for all three of them." *Jack's dad is still weeping and can't seem to talk, but he has already spoken to my heart and given me words of encouragement during the service. Slowly, so slowly, they leave the room.*

Now, no one is left but my little Isaac, my Jacob and dear Jack. As I watch them stand next to my lifeless body, the boys sobbing and Jack attempting to comfort them, all my self-centered decisions play out before me. How could I, as a wife and mother, have been so caught up with me?

As the three of them hold on to each other for strength and comfort, little Isaac is the first to speak.

"Mom, you can't leave me. I need you. Who will tuck me in at night? Who will pack my lunch for school? Who will bake cookies for Jacob and me? Mom, who will rub my head when I'm sick and wipe my face with a cold washcloth? Oh, Mom, who is going to pick out my clothes for school? Was it my fault Mom? What did I do? Why did you leave me?"

My little Isaac has reached his end. He can't talk anymore. Oh, dear God, how could I have left him in this dark emptiness? If only he could hear me, I would tell him how sorry I am for my selfishness. I would assure him he did nothing to deserve this. Will it be possible for me to help little Isaac from where I am? OH, HOW I DESPERATELY WANT TO!

Jacob's face is red and swollen from the trauma of the past few days. He looks as if he will explode from the inner pain he can't express. Jacob, my first born, you are strong willed and so gifted. I know your pain is deep. I know you are searching for the words to express what you are feeling, but maybe those words don't exist for you right now. Oh, Jacob, you are angry with me and your anger is so justified. Please don't suppress it—don't keep it inside. It's okay to tell me what you're feeling. As if he can hear me, Jacob's pain comes out in anger and he begins to speak.

"Mom, how could you do this? How could you run off and leave Dad? What has he ever done to you? How could you leave Isaac and me like that? Didn't you love us? We're just kids and we need a mom! I'll <u>never</u> understand! I'll <u>never</u> forgive you for what you've done! I'm <u>never</u> getting married! I hate you!"

Oh, precious Jacob. I'm so very sorry for the pain I've caused you. I hope someday you'll be able to forgive me. Don't let it destroy you, son.

Jack's mother is standing in the doorway motioning for Isaac and Jacob to come with her, leaving their dad to say his final goodbye to me. I know the boys don't want to leave him—or me. They're walking so slowly to their grandmother—confused and with broken hearts, their little bodies weighed down with grief. I watch as she wraps her loving arms around them and gently guides them to the front door. I'm so thankful for her and I know she will be there for my sons and their dad.

Jack has watched Isaac and Jacob leave and now turns to face the casket. With our boys gone from the room, his emotions finally pour out and he begins to sob. Jack's trying to speak, but I can't understand what he's saying because he's crying so hard and the words are stuck in his throat. My heart aches as I watch him struggle to talk. I wish I could hold him in my arms and comfort him. I know there's something he wants to tell me. I'm here, Jack, and ready to listen to whatever it is you want to say. As his sobs finally subside, he calms down enough to speak.

"Foreknown, there are so many things I need to tell you—things in my life that make me want to ask for your forgiveness. I hope I can make some sense of it all.

"I should have been there for you from the beginning, back in high school. If I had stood by you and taken responsibility for the pregnancy, maybe you wouldn't have had the abortion." *Did he say abortion? How did he...how long has he known?* "I've not been faithful to you either. The reality is, my unfaithfulness was more harmful to our marriage than yours. While I was climbing the ladder of success and trying to please everyone else, I had too little time for you. Looking back, I see how lonely and hurt you must have been. Sexual sins are not the only sins of unfaithfulness, Foreknown. When we got married, I was supposed to be single minded toward you and focused on you. Because I didn't give you that dedication, you searched elsewhere for it. Your search should have ended with me, but I wasn't there to be found. When I was growing up, I built walls around myself to protect me from the hurts of life. Those walls kept the hurts out, but they kept love out, too. They ended up keeping you out, Foreknown. Your needs were never met because I wouldn't let you in. Please forgive me." *Oh, Jack, I do forgive you. Please don't cry. I wish I could hold you and make everything all right.*

"My life has been such a mess. There is so much you never knew about me. When we were dating, I began to hang out with some people in school I shouldn't have been around. I started smoking pot and never stopped. During the years of our marriage, instead of facing problems head on with the help of the Lord, I sedated them with drugs. Just before I built our house, I was offered some crack cocaine. I willingly opened that 'door' and my life changed in a horribly negative way. The drug controlled me and, because of it, I was sexually unfaithful to you, too. Then, when we moved into our new house, I found someone who shared my drug habit. Many times, while you and Sharon were out shopping, Leonard and I were getting high. We were Christians but living another whole life. I was only able to keep all of this hidden from you because you were so focused on your own life and looking for someone who would satisfy the deep emotional needs you longed to have met. Because I am so weak, sometimes the drugs still control me. I need help. I promise you I <u>will</u> get help—not just for me, but for the sake of our sons. Oh, Foreknown, I am asking you and the Lord to please forgive me." *I do, Jack. I do forgive you. How I wish I'd known about your struggle. You're so right, Jack. I had no idea. I was so self-absorbed and consumed by my own needs.*

"During our marriage, I knew about a lot of things you were doing, but I always made the choice not to confront you. By failing to do that, I never gave us a chance to try to work through our problems. I kept waiting for you to come to me. I knew about the lovers because our phones were tapped and I had you followed. I knew about the abortions because I answered calls from Dr. Slaughter. At one point my anger was out of control because of the choices we were both making. Trying to work through our problems would have been useless. I had no room for forgiveness… I was carrying such a grudge. Because of that, there was so much I purposely withheld from you. I was angry and desperately wanted to get even with you. I've been so wrong. I know we could have worked through everything if we had just been honest with each other. Foreknown, please forgive me. Lord, please forgive me." *I forgive you, Jack. I only hope you can forgive me—and that God will forgive us both.*

"As a little boy growing up, I had such dreams of a great, godly marriage. How did it come to this? I have carried so much anger toward you and guilt and shame toward myself for not being a godly man. I know there must be some black secret, some unfulfilled desire that took you away from me so many times. I wish I had talked with you and been what you needed. I wish I had gained your trust so you would have talked to me." *Oh, how I wish I would have, Jack.* "I used to tell you that you were beautiful and how I loved to kiss you and hold you in my arms." *I remember.* "Why didn't I keep telling you those things? They were still true." *Oh, Jack.*

"There are so many things I don't understand. If there is a God, there has to be a reason and a good purpose for bringing us to this dark and horrible moment. Oh, Foreknown, my sweet Foreknown, we have destroyed ourselves and each other. Now, the only hope I have is in the Lord." *He is my only hope, too, Jack.* "I am trusting Him for strength and courage to go on and that eternity will reveal the answers to the questions of this life.

"I'll watch over our sons and love them for both of us. Give Jacob some time. I know he'll forgive you. I'll work with him. Right now, he's angry and confused—all three of us are. It's so difficult to believe this has happened to our little family." *I'm sorry, Jack... so very sorry!*

"Now, here I am—alone and realizing I'll never again in this life hold you or kiss your lips. I'll never be able to reach for your hand again. We'll never go to church together again. You won't be coming home with us or be waiting there for us. We won't share a meal again or talk about the boys' school and their soccer games. I can't tell you about my aches and pains or share my fears, my insecurities. You won't be there to laugh with me, or cry with me, or just be silent with me. You're gone, Foreknown. You're gone! I can hardly believe it. I wish I could go back and do things differently. There is so much I took for granted." *I did, too, Jack...so much.*

"The boys are waiting for me, Foreknown. I have to say goodbye. I want you to know I've forgiven you." *Thank you for this gift, Jack. It's so much more than I deserve.* "I have no more anger and no grudges to hold against you. Please feel free from all guilt and meet me at the gate when my time comes to enter that great city where there is no time, where we'll never say goodbye again, where tears and sadness are unknown." *Oh, I want to be there, Jack! I want to be there waiting for you! I hope I am!* "I know in heaven all our troubles will have passed and both of us will never hurt again. I'm resting in God's promises that we won't do battle with our flesh anymore and because of Jesus, we won't need to fear condemnation. "

Jack has stopped talking now. He has poured out everything that's in his heart. He looks empty but at peace. He hesitates, then bends over and kisses my lips. Oh, how I wish I could feel his lips on mine one more time. I took those kisses for granted for so many years. He's turning to leave the room, but it looks like he can hardly bring himself to go. The burden he's carrying, the one I've caused, is so heavy he can barely put one foot in front of another. I'm hurting for him. I don't want him to leave me. I want him to stay, but I know he can't. I watch him go to where our boys are. When he is within their reach, they grab him so tightly it looks as if they'll never let go. Hang on to him, sons! Hang on tight! Hold on to them, Jack! I watch them slowly walk to the car, supporting each other to be able to stand.

I am certainly worthy of eternal damnation, but my father-in-law's message still rings in my ears. There is this grace, this amazing grace, this free grace, this God-giving love for a 'Gomer' like me. Thank you, Jesus, for allowing me to hear the gospel one last time before my trial in Heaven. My father-in-law told me to sing. I remember a song from my childhood in that little Methodist church we attended. How did it go again?

> "And can it be that I should gain
> An interest in the Savior's blood?
> Died He for me, who caused His pain—
> For me, who Him to death pursued?
> Amazing love! How can it be,
> That Thou, my God, shouldst die for me?
> No CONDEMNATION now I dread;
> Jesus, and all in Him, is mine;
> Alive in Him, my living Head,
> And clothed in righteousness divine,
> Bold I approach th' eternal throne,
> And claim the crown, through Christ my own."

I wonder how the composer could have written such a hymn, unless, like me, he suffered from the terrible awareness of how awful our sin is before a holy God.

The Beginning of Life...Eternal

*S*uddenly, *I am summoned by a holy angel who transports me to another place. Not sure of exactly where I am, I wait for my senses to adjust to the sights and sounds of this place. As awareness of my surroundings settles in, my eyes observe a most unbelievable scene. I'm in a massive courtroom filled with more people than I've ever seen gathered in one place. They all appear to be on edge and restless,*

Curious as to exactly what's happening, I approach one of the court officers and ask, 'What's going on here? Why is there such excitement?'

"It is an important day in the High Court of Heaven," *he answers.* "This ocean of people, too great to number, has been assembled to stand before El-Shaddai, the Judge of the Ages—the Great One who cannot but know what is right and, thus, cannot but do what is just. We are awaiting the arrival of a special one. She will be the archetype for all those to follow—the ones who have been redeemed. Her conviction or acquittal will be the Judge's standard for the rest."

'*Who is the 'special one'?' I ask.*

"Her name is Foreknown Elect," *he answers.*

'*But... that's me!' I exclaim.*

"You are Foreknown Elect?" *the officer asks.*

'*Yes! I am!'*

"Come with me."

I follow him as he takes me directly to the clerk's desk to register for immediate trial.

As the realization of what is happening sets in, I begin to shake and am frightened beyond anything I've ever felt before! The terror within me of pending condemnation is indescribable! The text Jack's father read at my funeral flashes through my mind and my heart cries out, 'Oh, God, enter NOT into judgment with me!'

As my eyes continue to take in the vast scene before me, I turn and ask the court officer to tell me the names of some of the others in the room.

"The two figures you see behind the first table are Mr. Law and Mr. Justice, the prosecuting attorneys. Behind the second table is the defender, who, for today's purposes, is referred to as 'The Advocate'. He will plead this case on behalf of all the accused who are gathered here. The one sitting alone off to the side is the star witness for the prosecution."

As I turn to see the identity of the 'star witness', I realize his face is all too familiar. Our eyes lock and I recoil in horror as I see someone who is much too easily recognizable to me. It is Lucifer! I turn away quickly! I cannot bear to look at his face any longer! He will be my destruction in this place! He knows everything I have done and will use it to see that I am damned to hell for all eternity! Overwhelming fear has now besieged every fiber of my being!

I lift my eyes to the front of the courtroom and there, behind the judge's bench, sits El Shaddai, the Judge of the Ages. I am awed to be in His presence. He knows all about me, too. I feel myself shrinking from the humiliation and embarrassment of my life. Have mercy on me, O, God!

The noise in the courtroom becomes a welcome distraction. I look over the crowd, realizing I recognize many of them from their stories in the Scriptures. As I listen to what each one is saying, I am humbled and encouraged by their testimonies.

I know that one is Lydia—the lady who's so finely dressed in purple. She is saying over and over again, "He opened my heart down by the riverside."

The dirty, smelly, unshaven man, who bears scars in both his hands, keeps repeating, "Oh, what a wonder that He saved me! He said to me as I hung beside him, 'Today shalt thou be with me in paradise.' " *He must be the thief who was crucified on a cross next to the Savior.*

The man standing over there, small in stature, who keeps talking about Jesus calling him down from a sycamore tree and coming to his house, must be Zaccheus. His story is so familiar from my childhood.

I see a woman whose face is covered with so much make-up she looks like a clown and the smell of cheap perfume surrounds her like a fog. Tears are running down her cheeks, as she talks to anyone who will listen. "I was caught in the actual act of adultery by the elders of my religion. They grabbed me and threw me down at His feet, expecting Him to condemn me according to the law. They would have stoned me, but He identified with me. He stooped down to where I was and said to them, 'He that is without sin among you, let him first cast a stone at her.' He wrote something in the sand then asked me where all of my accusers were. Amazed, I told Him I had none—they were gone! Then He spoke those wonderful words to me, 'NEITHER DO I CONDEMN THEE: GO, AND SIN NO MORE.' "

I am immersed in their testimonies, when my attention is suddenly diverted by a Mr. Gabriel, who is crying out:

"Hear, ye! Hear, ye! The High Court of Heaven is now in session...The Honorable El Shaddai presiding."

<u>Judge El Shaddai pounds the gavel and speaks</u>:

"This court is now in session. Mr. Law and Mr. Justice, you may call your first witness."

Mr. Law calls Mr. Lucifer to the stand.

<u>Mr. Law</u>:

"Mr. Lucifer, are you acquainted with all of the accused?"

<u>Mr. Lucifer</u>:

"I am well acquainted with <u>all</u> of these people. I have been in their homes, their cars, their bars and I have an intimate knowledge of each and every one of them. In fact, they were all friends of mine at one time. We worked together and they walked according to my direction. They reveled in their lusts and fulfilled every desire of the flesh and of the mind. They are as guilty as I and by nature deserve wrath. Mrs. Elect, in particular, is a wretched representative of this throng and has proven herself to be ignorant and easily deceived. There are many things I can reveal about her that this court may not know. Would you like to ask me about her?"

I shudder to hear my name come out of his mouth! He deceived me, but I participated willingly. I am so repulsed by him now!

<u>Mr. Law responds, ignoring the last question:</u>

"I have no further questions for this witness, your Honor."

<u>Judge El Shaddai speaks:</u>

"My Son, do you have any questions for this witness?"

Wait! Did He say, 'my son'? Yes, I'm sure that's what He said. If that's true, Judge El Shaddai is The Advocate's father. And if my defender is the judge's son that can only be good for my case!

<u>The Advocate answers:</u>

"Yes, my Father."

<u>The Advocate proceeds with Mr. Lucifer:</u>

"Just so you know, there is nothing about Mrs. Elect this court does not know. I do, however, have some questions for you, Mr. Lucifer. Isn't it true you are a known rebel and liar? Isn't it true you tried your best to kill El Shaddai, the judge in this very case, and His Holy Son? Mr. Lucifer, isn't it true you and your myriads were thrown out of heaven for insurrection?"

Lucifer, although visibly irritated, attempts to remain calm and answers:

"Well, yes, I purposed to ascend into heaven and exalt my throne above the stars of God. I said I would sit upon the mount of the congregation in the sides of the north. I wanted to be like the Most High. I would have accomplished my purpose had not El Shaddai been sovereign. Why, 'none can stay his hand, or say unto him, What doest thou?' 'I was brought down to hell, to the sides of the pit.' "

The Advocate continues questioning:

"Mr. Lucifer, isn't it true you yourself have been tried and convicted of high treason? Isn't it also true you have already been sentenced to eternal hell and at this very moment are shackled in chains?"

Mr. Lucifer responds in a threatening manner:

"Advocate, that is true, but count on this: If El Shaddai or His Son ever grow weak, I will be back!"

<u>The Advocate moves on</u>:

"Lucifer, you testified you knew all of these accused people—that they were all with you at one time. Isn't it true, however, that a phenomenon occurred within them and they, for some strange reason, became ill every time you drew near? They no longer wanted to go where you once went or do what you did. Isn't it true they sickened of your company?"

<u>Mr. Lucifer</u>:

"Yes, and I know why. The spirit of the Most High came upon them in life-giving power and threw me out of them—so they could not do the things they once did. Then the grace of God kept teaching them to deny ungodliness and worldly lust and to live soberly and righteously in this present evil world."

<u>The Advocate charges the witness stand</u>:

"And you, Lucifer, accuse my brethren . . ."

My brethren? Why would He use that term?

"...day and night. But isn't it true an investigation has been made by the most holy and reliable sources and not a shred of evilness has surfaced? In fact, only a positive righteousness has prevailed. Isn't it true a search warrant was issued by Judge El Shaddai and served by Mr. Law and Mr. Justice—a search that actually took place for their sins on earth, in the heavens, in hell itself and none could be found?"

Mr. Lucifer cries out:

"Search again! Someone has tampered with the books! I was with them! I promoted the most wicked of sins and encouraged each one in their rebellion to commit them! I <u>know</u> they committed them! I was daily with Mrs. Elect. Why, I was with her in the plane just before this trial began. Surely you saw it."

What?! No! Please, stop! I can't bear to think The Advocate or anyone else in this room saw that! I just want all of this to be finished!

The Advocate speaks, ignoring Mr. Lucifer's last statement:

"I have one final question for you, Lucifer. How did you acquire that terrible scar which leads us to believe your head may have been crushed at one time?"

Lucifer is visibly shaken and refuses to answer. Judge El Shaddai motions for Mr. Gabriel to help the weak and failing Lucifer down from the witness stand. He now seems confused and disoriented and is holding his head as if he is in the throes of a violent headache.

The scar! Of course! Another piece of the puzzle has fallen into place! It must have been from the crushing blow God promised would be inflicted on him when Jesus defeated death at Calvary, a promise going all the way back to the Garden of Eden!

<u>Judge El Shaddai speaks to the prosecutors</u>:

"You may call your next witness."

The two prosecuting attorneys turn toward each other and, unexpectedly, Mr. Justice calls Mr. Law to the stand.

<u>Mr. Justice speaks</u>:

"Now, Mr. Law, isn't it true you require perfect obedience in thought, word and deed? And isn't it true sin is disobedience of the law? Isn't it also true, Mr. Law, that Mrs. Elect and all the accused have sinned and fallen short of the righteousness demanded by the law and are worthy of nothing other than condemnation?"

<u>Mr. Law responds matter-of-factly</u>:

"Yes, Mr. Justice, all of those things are true and I'm sure the Honorable El Shaddai will agree. The accused have not manifested the perfect righteousness demanded; but, at best, all their 'righteousnesses are as filthy rags'. I have a list of 14 indictments against them:

1) None of them are righteous, truthful or upright—no, not a one.

2) None of them understood. Not one of them intelligently discerned or comprehended.

3) None of them, by their own dead will, sought God. El Shaddai, you know that!

4) They have all strayed from the way of righteousness.

5) There is not one of them who is worthy in and of themselves. They are worthless dung!

6) Not one of them is good. They talk about being 'pretty good', 'real good' and 'not as bad as others', but they are all liars. Furthermore, 'real good' or 'pretty good' is not what is demanded. Perfect righteousness is what I demand. They have never heard me make mention of 'partial' obedience, nor have I said anything of 'sincere' obedience. There is nothing in me about sincerity—not a word. I have never even hinted at such a thing. I demand

perfect, uncompromising obedience and an absolute conformity to the law in thought, word and deed. I know no righteousness, except that which is perfect.

7) Their throats are open sepulchers—yawning graves.

8) They use their tongues to deceive, to mislead and to deal treacherously. Mrs. Elect is a prime example. She was a master of deception.

I cringe at the mention of my name again and the accusations against me. The fear I have been attempting to suppress seems to be taking over every part of me.

9) The poison of snakes is under their lips.

10) Their mouths are full of cursing and bitterness.

11) Their feet are swift to shed blood.

12) Destruction and misery mark their ways.

13) They have no experience in the way of peace. They know nothing about peace, for a peaceful way they do not even recognize.

14) There is no fear of God before their eyes.

"I speak as an authority. It is evident all of the accused have sinned. They are transgressors and are worthy of condemnation. I <u>cannot</u> and <u>will</u> <u>not</u> ignore a single sin!"

Mr. Justice asks:

"Are you saying, Mr. Law, the accused broke the law with willful intent—that Mrs. Elect went after her lovers with purpose and planning?"

Stop! Please, stop!

Mr. Law replies:

"Most certainly, Mr. Justice. They all did what they did with willful intent; because, when they knew God, and recognized Him as God, they did not honor or glorify Him as God, or give thanks to Him. Instead, they became futile and godless in their thinking, with vain imaginings, foolish reasoning and stupid speculations. Their senseless minds were darkened."

Mr. Justice asks:

"Mr. Law, what is it you ask of this court?"

Mr. Law responds:

"I demand that every one of the accused silence their excuses and plead guilty before El Shaddai! Their deeds have in no way justified them. Their tears of sorrow for the past will not satisfy me, nor will reforming their future. I told them, 'Do this or you shall surely die' and they are cursed because they did not continue in all things pertaining to the law."

Mr. Justice ends:

"Your honor, I have no further questions for this witness,"

Judge El Shaddai speaks:

"My Son, The Advocate, do you have any questions of this witness for the defense."

Again, He says, 'my Son'! My heart beats faster at the sound of those words!

The Advocate answers:

"Yes, my Father."

Confirmation! He <u>did</u> say 'my Father'. Could it be there is a holy conspiracy taking place right here in the high court of heaven?

<u>The Advocate begins</u>:

"Mr. Law, you never attempted to make the accused what they should be, did you? And isn't it true that you, Mr. Law, could not make them right with you because of the weakness of their flesh? I realize the failure is not your fault, Mr. Law. You were on their conscience and the accused were well aware of your principle rule: 'Do this and you shall be rewarded, do that and you shall be punished.' We all know what you have said and that it must be enforced—the accused must produce a perfect righteousness. If not, 'The soul that sinneth, it shall die'. We all agree in this court that the law is unalterable and the accused have broken the law. Let us suppose, however, some infinitely perfect active obedience, which would be effective for all of eternity, took place on behalf of the sinners and the law was magnified and made honorable. Would you then be satisfied, Mr. Law?"

<u>Mr. Law nods in agreement and answers</u>:

"Most certainly, I would. If there could be found an active obedience to the law, a keeping and fulfilling of it by someone who could answer all the demands I have made upon the accused, then I shall be satisfied."

<u>The Advocate asks</u>:

"Mr. Law, are you aware of the meaning of the name, 'Jehovah-jireh?'"

In spite of the numbing fear within me, suddenly, I'm all ears! The light of gospel truth preached at my funeral is beginning to dawn in my soul and my mind asks with Charles Wesley,

> "And can it be that I should gain
> An interest in the Savior's blood?
> Died He for me, who caused His pain—
> For me, who Him to death pursued?
> Amazing love! How can it be
> That Thou, my God, shouldst die for me?"

<u>Mr. Law replies</u>:

"Yes, of course. It means 'the Lord will provide'."

<u>The Advocate goes on</u>:

"Mr. Law, are you aware of any such provision being made on behalf of the accused ones by El Shaddai?"

Mr. Law hesitates, then responds:

"Well, yes. I know what I could not do because of the weakness of the flesh of the accused, <u>God</u> did by sending His own Son in the likeness of sinful man to be a sin offering, 'condemning sin in the flesh'."

The Advocate continues:

"Now, Mr. Law, you have just stated what <u>you</u> could <u>not</u> do, <u>God</u> <u>did</u> by sending 'His own Son in the likeness of sinful flesh, and for sin, condemned sin in the flesh'. Is that correct?"

Mr. Law agrees:

"Yes, that's correct, Advocate."

The Advocate asks:

"Now, Mr. Law, where, specifically, did God send His Son?"

Mr. Law replies:

"Well, first God sent His Son to earth, to Bethlehem to be born into the human race. Then He sent His Son to Calvary to die a human death. Finally, He sent His Son down to the grave, but then recalled Him to His own right hand, where he makes intercession today."

The Advocate probes further:

"And why did He send His Son, Mr. Law?"

Mr. Law readily answers:

"He was sent to come under the jurisdiction of the law and to meet every demand of it right down to crossing the t's and dotting the i's, then to condemn and destroy sin—to put it away, to make an end of it."

The Advocate continues:

"So, the Son of God was not sent to be a lawgiver, but a Savior. He was not sent to spy out the sins of these accused ones but to deliver the accused from bondage and condemnation. Are those statements correct, Mr. Law?"

Mr. Law responds:

> "Those statements are correct, Advocate. He was sent to earth to do those very things. He is a friend of sinners—the lowest of the low."

The Advocate asks:

> "Mr. Law, can you tell the court the name of this Savior?"

Mr. Law replies:

> "I most certainly can! His name is 'JESUS: for He shall save His people from their sins.'"

Oh, the sweet name of Jesus! How lovely it is to my ears!

The Advocate:

> "Now, Mr. Law, you have already testified that sin is the disobedience of the law. Correct?"

Mr. Law:

> "That is correct, Advocate."

The Advocate:

"So, Mr. Law, the accused are law breakers and have not produced what you demanded, which is perfect obedience and ongoing righteousness."

Mr. Law:

"That is correct. They have not produced a perfect righteousness."

The Advocate:

"Now, Mr. Law, let's go back to the matter of God sending His own Son to do what you could not do because of the weakness of the flesh on the part of the accused. Isn't it true that by the obedience of this one, this Jesus, many have been made righteous?"

Mr. Law:

"Mr. Justice and I were discussing this very matter before the trial began. It would seem there is a number no man can number, of every kindred, tongue and nation, whose records show a positive righteousness, even the righteousness of God's own Son, which has been imputed, or accredited, to their account. I have been told the Honorable El Shaddai possesses a book with the names of these people recorded therein. This mysterious book is known in heavenly circles as 'The Lamb's Book of Life'. It is a book of antiquity dating back to before the beginning of time and the names recorded on its pages were written there before the foundation of the world."

<u>The Advocate turns to the Judge and says</u>:

"My Father, I have no further questions for this witness at this time."

He continues to refer to the judge as 'my Father'. In my heart I feel such comfort from those words, but it's still confusing to me. I don't understand why The Advocate is referring to El Shaddai as 'Father'.

<u>Judge El Shaddai speaks</u>:

"Mr. Law, you may step down."

A rumor is being circulated in the celestial halls that all parties involved in this trial are well aware of its outcome with the exception of the accused, who continually doubt their acquittal. There is one, however, who seems to be gaining confidence—a confidence verging on blessed assurance. The fear in Foreknown Elect is slowly dissipating, being replaced with a quiet calmness, which is becoming obvious to all in the room.

<u>Judge El Shaddai continues speaking</u>:

"You may call your next witness, Mr. Law."

Mr. Law calls Mr. Justice to the witness stand.

<u>Mr. Law</u>:

"Mr. Justice, now that we have established guilt on the part of the accused, what is it you demand of these transgressors of the law?"

<u>Mr. Justice cries out</u>:

"I <u>demand</u> their execution, the only outcome which would render satisfaction! I will settle for nothing less than complete appease-ment for the sins of the accused! It is the law, as you well know! I cannot sheath my sword until I have inflicted the threatened curse for the breaking of the law by the accused! I must see the sentence of the law fully executed! I am vindictive and full of wrath!"

Mr. Law:

"Is there anything the accused could have done to deliver themselves? Could they have offered anything to you, Mr. Justice, to save themselves from the wages of sin—perhaps if they said they were sorry for their sins and wept and mourned bitterly?"

Mr. Justice shakes his head as he replies in astonishment:

"I couldn't begin to count the times I've heard Mrs. Elect weep and mourn with bitterness over her mess-ups! She, along with the rest of the accused, would accomplish nothing more than openly confessing their guilt by doing that! It would be an acknowledgement of their deserved penalty!"

Mr. Law:

"Now, Mr. Justice, isn't it true that in the past you held the accused hostage because they could not meet the ransom demands?"

Mr. Justice:

"Well, yes, at that time they were held because they were transgressors of the law and the law is unalterable. It was the law that sentenced them. So, I held them until the penalty could be inflicted upon them—the penalty being the second death."

Mr. Law:

"I have no further questions for this witness, your Honor."

Judge El Shaddai asks:

"My Son, do you have any questions for Mr. Justice?"

The Advocate:

"Yes, my Father."

This Father appears to be very well pleased with His Son, but it continues to be puzzling to me why a judge and a defender would use such familiar terms with each other, especially in a setting like this.

The Advocate:

"Mr. Justice, I am well aware the accused could not stay their deserved punishment. But let us suppose there were some infinitely meritorious sufferings someone would undergo in the sinners' stead. If someone answered all the demands Law and

Justice required from Mrs. Elect and the rest of the accused, would you then be satisfied?"

Mr. Justice:

"How could I not be satisfied if there was an acceptable substitute who would come alongside the accused and bear their sins, guilt and punishment? But I must ask you: If a man sins against the Lord, who would intercede for him? I know for a fact there was certainly no help for the accused on earth. I also know that no creature in Heaven, even among the highest order of the angels, could deliver any <u>one</u> sinner from his distress, much less a multitude like this. I think I could safely say no eye would have pitied them if it was not for 'Grace'."

The Advocate begins to gently question in another direction:

"Mr. Justice, I'm sure you have experienced love. In fact, my sources tell me you have been seen embracing and kissing 'Peace'. I believe you, Mr. Justice, live daily in complete satisfaction with 'Peace', who is caring and comforting toward all the accused. Am I correct?"

Mr. Justice:

"Yes. What you have said is true, Advocate."

The Advocate continues questioning:

"Further, Mr. Justice, aren't you in fact wedded to 'Peace' and didn't this union take place over 2000 years ago outside Jerusalem on Mt. Calvary? Also, isn't it true that 'Mercy' and 'Truth' were witnesses to this wedding?"

Mr. Justice responds:

"Yes, yes, the four of us, 'Mercy', 'Truth', 'Peace' and I have loved each other for eons. I first caught 'Peace's' eye before the beginning of time at the council table, where the Father, Son and Holy Spirit formed an eternal covenant of grace and love. The next time we saw each other was in the Garden of Eden after the fall of man. Discouraged, we parted company there, but met again at Bethlehem. What a great time that was..."

As if he is remembering, Mr. Justice's voice trails off for a moment, then continues:

"Yes, it's true we were wed at Calvary, when the punishment of the accused ones was upon Him and He was the only road to 'Peace'. I would like to add, Mr. Law and 'Mercy' were also wed that day."

The Advocate:

"Has there ever been a time, since your union with 'Peace' at Calvary, when you felt the need to put her away, divorce her and take up your sword of Justice again?"

Mr. Justice:

"Advocate, 2000 years ago, when 'Peace' and I were seen kissing, it was the day we were wed. 'The Peacemaker' had just concluded our union by saying, 'It is finished'. I shall never forget the rush of total satisfaction that filled me. All wrath and disapproval were gone. There was nothing left in me but ever-lasting satisfaction and righteousness."

The Advocate:

"As a reminder, Mr. Justice, during Mr. Law's interrogation, you stated you held the accused captive as sentenced law breakers. Since Mr. Law and 'Mercy' are wed and you, Mr. Justice, are wed to 'Peace', it would seem you have no right to hold them."

Mr. Justice:

"It's strange you should bring that up. It was at the conclusion of the union between 'Peace' and myself, immediately after 'The Peacemaker' said, 'It is finished', that we heard a holy voice from Heaven, much like the voice of El Shaddai, saying, 'Deliver them from going down to the pit—I have found a ransom'. Immediately, I gave up all of the accused…willingly, justly and righteously."

The Advocate:

"My Father, I have no further questions for this witness."

Judge El Shaddai speaks:

"Mr. Law and Mr. Justice you may call your next witness."

<u>Mr. Law and Mr. Justice</u>:

"Your Honor, we call Foreknown Elect to the stand."

I am startled to hear my name called; but as I walk toward the witness stand, I feel an inner calmness coming from the very depth of me and spreading itself throughout my being. The fear that had been so threatening to me is now gone. I have been strengthened by The Advocate's line of questioning.

<u>Mr. Law begins the interrogation</u>:

"Please state your full name for the court."

<u>Foreknown Elect responds calmly</u>:

"My full name is Foreknown Elect, which means, foreloved and chosen, but some refer to me as 'Sought-out'."

<u>Mr. Law</u>:

"Mrs. Elect, you seem to have grown in boldness during this Day of Judgment. When I observed you at the beginning of this trial, you appeared to be worried and filled with fear. Later, I overheard you whisper to one of the angelic beings present that you feel a deep assurance when The Advocate takes the floor in defense of the accused. Why is that?"

Foreknown Elect responds:

"Mr. Law, when love is within us, 'we may have boldness in the Day of Judgment: because as He is, so are we'. 'Perfect love casteth out fear'. I love The Advocate, 'because He first loved' me."

Mr. Law asks:

"Mrs. Elect, may I call you by your first name?"

Foreknown Elect responds:

"Yes, of course, Mr. Law. Now that I understand you and I have been best of friends for over 2000 years since your marriage to 'Mercy', please call me by my first name."

Mr. Law:

"Thank you. Now, Foreknown, isn't it true you came out of your mother's womb speaking lies; like an unwanted infant your navel was not cut; you weren't washed with water or powdered and clothed; there was no one who pitied you; you were a despised thing who was thrown in an open field and lay there covered in your own blood, devoid of strength? Isn't it also true, like Mephibosheth in the days of old, your growing up years were spent down in Lo-debar? While there, did you not waste all you had and all you were by living a reckless life? Were there not days without number when you wallowed in the mire of a hog pen, eating corn husks with the pigs like the prodigal son? Isn't it true, Foreknown, like Gomer, you were engaged to one who was holy, spotless and undefiled? Yet, while being engaged to Him, you went after other lovers and became a whore? Isn't it true while on earth you were spotted and blemished, at one time even being referred to as a 'dead dog'?"

Foreknown Elect, tears welling in her eyes, responds sadly:

"All you have said of me is true, sir."

Mr. Law yields to Mr. Justice, who steps forward and asks:

"May I, too, call you by your first name?"

Foreknown Elect:

"Yes, Mr. Justice. But before you go on, I want to tell you what a wonderful woman your wife is. 'Peace'...she truly surpasses all understanding."

Mr. Justice continues questioning for the prosecution:

"Thank you, Foreknown. Am I correct in stating while on earth you said you did what you did not want to do, and what you wanted to do you didn't, and what you hated you did? Is it not your very own confession that in your flesh nothing good existed?"

Foreknown Elect:

"Mr. Justice, all you have said of me while I was on earth is true; but even then, though my life was black with sin, I was beautiful in the eyes of God."

Mr. Justice:

"Your honor, Mr. Law and I have no further questions for this witness."

Judge El Shaddai speaks:

"Advocate, my Son, do you have any questions for my beloved Foreknown?"

Foreknown's eyes are fixed on 'The Advocate' as He approaches the witness stand, gently takes her hand in His and speaks to her in terms filled with affection and gentle assurance.

"You are beautiful. You are all fair, my love, my Foreknown. There is not a spot or blemish about you. I am so happy to have you here where I am. I prayed for this day to come. I want you to know your winter is past. The rain is over and gone. It is now and forever a time of blooming flowers and cooing doves. The season of singing has come for you, my love, my fair one. Mr. Lucifer, Mr. Law and Mr. Justice have all made accusations against you and I want you to give them your response. I know you have an answer for the hope within you, don't you? Mr. Law said from birth you were unclean, your navel wasn't cut, neither were you washed nor powdered and clothed. You were thrown in an open field and lay there in your own blood, unwanted and devoid of strength. Do you have anything to say to these charges?"

<u>As Foreknown Elect is now realizing the true identity of The Advocate, she responds eagerly</u>:

"Oh, Advocate, all Mr. Law has said is true with the exception that no one pitied me. There was one, beloved Advocate, who looked upon me, polluted in my sins, and said to me, 'Live'! It was a time of incredible love. He spread His robe of righteousness over me and covered my nakedness. He swore He would never leave me nor forsake me. He said, 'You are mine'. He washed me thoroughly with water, cleansing away the blood-stains of sin from me. He anointed me with oil. He clothed me in beautiful embroidered cloth and gave me walking shoes. He gave me a belt of fine linen, covered me with silk and adorned me with ornaments and bracelets and chains. He put a jewel on my forehead, earrings in my ears and a beautiful crown on my head. I have no self defense for my sinful nature. I can only say there was one who loved me despite my natural depravity. He was the only one who loved me enough to do something about my condition."

<u>The Advocate asks</u>:

"Is this one, who is so full of graciousness, in the courtroom today and do you recognize Him? Do you know his voice?"

Foreknown Elect responds:

"Oh, yes! I know his voice! He is the only one my soul loves! The voice of another I will not hear."

The Advocate:

"Foreknown, thou fairest among women, Mr. Law spoke of you being down in Lo-debar, living a reckless life, eating husks with pigs. What do you have to say for yourself with regard to these accusations?"

Foreknown Elect:

"I can only say Mr. Law's accusations were all true. I was in Lo-debar, a place of no bread, wallowing in the filth of swine. My soul was wasting away on the husks the pigs ate and no one gave anything to me. But there was an effectual summons, issued by one who loved me before I knew Him, to fetch me out of Lo-debar. He sent His own Son to my wilderness to speak comfortably to me and we came out of the wilderness together, me leaning on my Beloved. From then on, I, the disfigured, husk-eating, dead dog, sat at the King's table continually, just as if I was one of his daughters!"

The Advocate:

"If called upon, could you point out the King and His Son who fetched you out of your black hole?"

Foreknown Elect:

"Oh, yes! I could never forget the day he came to me. I was at the dung hill, scrounging around for a morsel, and He came to me. When I could not go to Him, He came to me."

The Advocate:

"Mr. Law brought it to our attention that during the engagement to your Beloved you became a whore. He said you were not single minded, that there was no exclusivity to your love. Is this true, Foreknown?"

Foreknown Elect cries out:

"Yes, yes, it's all true! I was destroying myself, but the one to whom I was engaged would not let me go—in Him was my help. He loved me freely and promised me to Himself forever. He promised me to Himself in righteousness and in judgment, in loving kindness and in mercy. He promised me to Himself in faithfulness and now I know only Him!"

The Advocate:

"Foreknown Sought-out Elect, is your loving Hosea in this courtroom?"

Foreknown Elect shouts:

"OH, PRECIOUS ADVOCATE, BLESSED INTERCESSOR, BREAD OF HEAVEN, WATER OF LIFE, LAMB OF GOD, IT IS YOU!!! It was you who came into the world at Bethlehem to do what Mr. Law could not do! It was you who came up under the law, keeping it for me! It was you who went to Calvary and took the curse upon yourself, bearing my sin and satisfying Mr. Justice! This court can <u>never</u> find me guilty, for there is no sin to be found! You, my Lord, made an end of sin! You removed it 'as far as the east is from the west'! You are the appointed man who carried my sins into the wilderness, the Lamb of God who has taken them all away, the one who said to me, 'Neither do I condemn thee'! Who can charge me with <u>anything</u>? I am El Shaddai's elect! It is you, my Advocate, who is the Christ that died for me, who is risen from the dead for me, who also, right now, intercedes for me in this courtroom! You are the sacrificial Lamb of Exodus 14 without spot, whose blood must be sprinkled on the two sides of the door frame! You are the ark of Noah's day and everyone in that ark is safe from the watery wrath of judgment! You are the good shepherd who left the 90 and 9 and sought the one lost sheep until you found it, put it on your shoulders and brought it safely to the fold! I ask you, Mr. Justice, do you have any vengeance to place on me or are you perfectly satisfied with me and see me justified? I ask you, Mr. Law, have I not met all your requirements through my Substitute, my Redeemer, my Advocate? I ask you, Mr. Justice, has my debt been paid to you in full? Are you my friend forevermore? I ask you, my Lord and Savior, to own me before El Shaddai!"

<u>The Advocate raises His eyes to the front of the courtroom and speaks to the Judge of the Ages</u>:

"Father, here am I, and the children You have given me."

What is happening now? El Shaddai has left the Judgment Throne and is walking toward me holding a holy white handkerchief in his large hands. What is He going to do? He is wiping away all my tears like a tender father would wipe the drops from the face of his darling daughter. He speaks and a warm, comforting wind moves through the courtroom.

<u>El Shaddai then speaks directly to me</u>:

"I want you to know, my little Elect, there shall be no more death, neither sorrow nor crying, neither shall there be any more pain; for the former things are passed away. I love you. I have always loved you. You are mine. You will never be condemned and you will never experience separation from my love."

I begin to praise Him!

"Thank you, Father God! Thank you, Lord Jesus! Thank you, Holy Spirit! Glory, Glory, to the Father! Glory, Glory to the Son! Glory, Glory to the Three in One! Thank you, Lord, for saving my soul! Thank you, Lord, for making me whole! Thank you, Lord, for giving to me salvation so rich and free! He brought me out of that horrible pit, out of the miry clay, and set my feet on the solid rock!"

I stand to my feet! I begin to do a holy dance and sing!

"'O, what a wonder that Jesus loves me. Out in the darkness no light could I see. O, what a wonder, He put His great arm under and wonder of wonders, He saved even me!' 'Amazing grace! How sweet the sound that saved a wretch like me! I once was lost, but now am found; was blind, but now I see!' "

I shout for all to hear!

"MY TRIAL IS OVER! I AM FOREVER FREE FROM CONDEMNATION, FOREVER FREE FROM GUILT, FOREVER FREE FROM SIN! THE COMFORTER HAS COME! I HAVE BEEN REDEEMED!"

The angels and seraphim can hold back no longer! The heavenly choir is on their feet, ten thousand times ten thousand of them, singing with a voice that rolls like a mighty thunder through the halls of Heaven! As they encircle the throne of El Shaddai, their voices rise as one, singing in beautiful harmony, in perfect pitch, with a sound that can only be heard in the heavenly realms!

"Worthy is the Lamb that was slain to receive glory and honor and praise now and forever!"

Since time is absent in Heaven, I have no concept of how long the choir has been singing. It is a sound like no other, one I've never heard before—no mortal ear can! How joyous! How wonderful! How can sheer joy be explained, other than SHEER JOY? That's all there is!

El Shaddai speaks to me again. At the sound of His voice, the beautiful, harmonic, heavenly singing seems to fade into the background.

"I desire for you to meet more of those who love you."

I can't imagine feeling any more loved than I do right now! At that moment, two children step around from behind El Shaddai. I don't know them, but they are so gorgeous to me. Wait! I DO know them! Yes! They are the beautiful babies I aborted...a darling girl and a handsome boy! They take my hands in theirs.

"Mommy, we want to tell you our names! You didn't give them to us, but God had them recorded in 'The Lamb's Book of Life' from the foundation of the world! I am your son, Peculiar, so named because God's people are a peculiar people. This is your little girl, Precious, so named because God's people are precious in His sight!"

Precious wraps her little arms around my leg and says,

"Oh, Mommy, I knew the trial would go well for you! Our Heavenly Father works everything for the good of them that love Him and are called according to His purpose! Come with us, Mommy! We want to show you the place Jesus has prepared for us!"

The children are so excited about all of us being together they just can't stop talking. They have been taught well by their Heavenly Father.

As we stroll down Grace Street, hand in hand, I begin to hear an indescribably sweet sound. Walking a little farther, I realize it sounds like the laughter of children—tens of thousands of them!

To be sure of what I'm hearing, I ask Precious and Peculiar:

"Is that the laughter of happy children?"

Peculiar answers, "Yes, we're almost to Grace Park. It's the largest park and the only one for children in all of Heaven—but there are children everywhere here, Mom. We can even play in the streets in Heaven!"

Rounding the corner, I see myriads of happy children—a throng of them beyond number!

I ask, "Where have all these children come from?"

"Well, Mommy," *Peculiar says,* "many of them came here because of abortion, like Precious and me. Some of them died of childhood diseases. Some just went to sleep in their little cribs and never woke up to their mother's smile again."

I realize he's describing SIDS...crib death. I know Heaven will one day relieve the horrible guilt so many mothers and fathers have carried who lost their precious babies that way.

"Some of these children were murdered by their own abusive parents," *Peculiar continues.* "Some were kidnapped and sold into child pornography...then murdered. There are some that had their lives taken from them while they were in the care of systems that were supposed to protect them."

Foster Care! How heartbreaking! Hearing Peculiar talk about what happened to some of these children makes me realize all Foster Care parents aren't like the ones I knew—kind and loving. The thought of it is too horrible to bear! All those precious innocents!

"Our Heavenly Father never intended for the 'state' to be parents."

We are still walking by the park when, ahead of us, a voice calls out to my children,

"Hey, Precious and Peculiar! Is this your mom?"

"Yes," *Peculiar answers.* "Mom, this is our friend, Stuart. His dad is the pastor of an inner-city church and his mom is the director at a Christian shelter for women and children. His parents are both still on earth, but Stuart is here because of a car accident. He wasn't even born yet. He came here from his mother's womb when she was 8 months pregnant."

"I'm so glad to meet you, Mrs. Elect!" *Stuart greets me with a bright, happy smile.* "If we weren't in Heaven, I would be jealous of Precious and Peculiar. I can hardly wait until my mom and dad are here with me! They hurt so much when I was taken from them, but I believe Heavenly Father knows what's best. I know my dad has said losing me made him a more compassionate pastor. I will introduce you to both of them when they get here. Have to go now! It sure is nice to finally meet Precious and Peculiar's mom. See you soon around Heavenly Father's throne in praise and worship!"

As we continue up Grace Street toward the home Jesus has prepared for us, I tell the children,

"I'm amazed at the army of little ones who are here."

Precious is quick to respond.

"Mommy, Heavenly Father loves children! Don't you remember? When He was on earth, He said, permit 'the little children to come unto me and forbid them not'. He says we are precious in His sight.

There are so many of us here, not because we are little ones, but because of the atoning blood of Jesus Christ. Maybe next time we visit the park I can introduce you to King David's little boy. We see him and his father a lot in the Throne Room in praise meetings."

This is so incredible to me! My children know people I've only read about in the Scriptures. They play with King David's son! Amazing!

As if she can read my next thought, Precious begins speaking to me about a subject that is weighing heavily on my mind.

"Mom, you might be having thoughts about who my father is. I know you feared the 'Choir Man' was my dad and that was the reason you aborted me. Mom, I want you to know Daddy Jack is my earthly father. I am here, you are here and Daddy Jack will be here soon, too! Isn't the grace of God marvelous, Mom?!"

"Yes, it is marvelous! Thank you, my darling, Precious."

I drop to my knees and envelop her in my arms. I hold her close to my heart for a long time, experiencing a feeling I robbed myself of while on earth—the overwhelming joy of holding my only daughter!

"Your dad is a man who knows and loves the Lord Jesus Christ. I believe when he gets here, he will discern all that has happened. He'll realize you are his daughter and he will love you as much as I do at this very moment."

EPILOGUE

A thousand years in time are like one day with the Lord—where there is no time. Back on earth, Maw Nanny has been a vital part of helping Jack and the boys cope with Foreknown's tragic death. She eventually shared with Jack that she suspected Foreknown's father had molested her and how she tried to approach Foreknown's mother, but was unable to help. Jack was stunned, but grateful Maw Nanny chose to share this, as it helped him reach a better understanding about some of the choices Foreknown made during her life. Jack loved Maw Nanny and often said she was one of the godliest women he had ever known and truly was a 'Mother in Israel'.

Within the year after Foreknown's funeral, her father's car was hit by a train at a railroad crossing. His earthly body was totally destroyed by the impact. The body of a 10-year-old girl, who was in the back seat of his car, was recovered from the scene of the accident. Jack and Maw Nanny attended the funeral of the little girl, a child lost in the state system. Foreknown's mother and father had become her foster parents. After the accident, Foreknown's mother had a mental and emotional breakdown and was institutionalized.

With God's help, Jack was able to overcome his drug addiction through a program for recovering addicts. Time passed and he began to spend time with Maw Nanny's daughter, Grace, who had so many of the same, sweet characteristics of her precious mother.

As for the boys...Jacob turned out to be an all-state football player in the high school where Jack had played so many years before. Jacob did practice in the hot August sun wearing the same gear as the rest of the guys. Isaac was a straight 'A' student, gifted in the arts. He loved music and was on his way to becoming an accomplished pianist.

Jack's parents were older now. They never recovered completely from Foreknown's death. Jack's father would often break down when talking about the guilt of sin and condemnation. He seemed at times to struggle greatly with living in a tainted, evil world. He would cry out during many of his sermons, seemingly under a load too difficult for him to carry, "Oh, the exceeding sinfulness of sin!" Jack's mother was a sweet grandmother, as well as a wonderful surrogate mother to the boys. She didn't miss a single one of Jacob's football games. A pianist herself at Graceville Reformed Baptist Church, she naturally was drawn to Isaac's gifts. At every one of his concerts, he could expect to see her proud, smiling face in the crowd. When either one of the boys received honors, all the people who loved them were there—Jack, Grace, Maw Nanny, Pastor Elect and First Lady, Mrs. Elect.

As Foreknown and her children continue up the main street in New Jerusalem, they see at the corner of Mercy and Grace a gorgeous mansion awaiting them. This is where they will spend heavenly moments waiting for the sound of the trumpet of God, the resurrection of the saints on earth and the changing of those who are still alive. Here, in the presence of the God who foreloved them, they will wait for their Jack, their Jacob, and their Isaac.